Twayne's United States Authors Series

SYLVIA E. BOWMAN, *Editor*

Indiana University

Edna St. Vincent Millay

Edna St. Vincent Millay

EDNA ST. VINCENT MILLAY

By NORMAN A. BRITTIN

University of Puerto Rico

TWAYNE PUBLISHERS

A DIVISION OF G. K. HALL & CO., BOSTON

TO RUTH
WHO HAS BEEN INVOLVED
AND INVALUABLE

About the Author

Norman A. Brittin, currently professor of English at Auburn University, received his Ph.D. from the University of Washington. In a teaching career spanning over twenty years, he has been on the faculties of the universities of Southern California, Washington, Chicago and (most recently) Puerto Rico. Dr. Brittin's own poetry has been published in many university-affiliated reviews and he was instrumental during the forties in forming a new poetry magazine, *Experiment*. His critical and scholarly work has appeared in the *Western Humanities Review, Sewanee Review, Antioch Review* and *Shakespeare Quarterly*.

Preface

SOME POETS lead retired and uneventful lives; others not only devote themselves to the composition of verse but take part in worldly activities of business, war, travel, politics, and councils of men. Such poets as Chaucer, Lord Byron, Matthew Arnold, William Morris, and Archibald MacLeish led active lives. So did Edna St. Vincent Millay; as early as 1924 Harriet Monroe commented on the crowded activity of the poet's youth. After her marriage, although Millay settled at Steepletop, in Austerlitz, New York, she traveled, lived in New York and Paris, gave readings all over the country, took part in the Sacco-Vanzetti protest, and responded vigorously to the impact of World War II. She became known not only as a "popular poet" but as a "public poet."

A definitive biography of Millay must wait until the material accumulated at Steepletop has been thoroughly studied. One may hope that her sister Norma Millay will provide such a work. In the meantime, because of an active life, her position as a "public poet," and the subjective nature of her work, a book on Millay's literary significance cannot be written without taking account of her life. In this study, the first three chapters are devoted, therefore, to biography.

Millay's manifold activities are doubtless related to her versatility. A woman with talents that afforded many possibilities for a career, she had musical training and might have been a pianist or a song-writer; she also had theatrical experience and might have become an actress. She could have succeeded in prose and did, in fact, publish short stories and satires.

Arthur DuBois analyzed Millay in terms of the precocious child, the poet, the woman, and the mystic. For each of these terms there is in Millay a corresponding and contrasting quality. For the child—suggesting innocence, wonder, and the need for special consideration—there is the tomboy and tease. Full of swagger and banter, she is a kind of Tom Sawyer who wants to do things in a "highfalutin" style. For the poet, full of lyrical feeling and sensitivity, there is the satirist. Ready with the wisecrack, she is the author of the Nancy Boyd sketches, and in her letters she frequently snaps a satirical lash and is indignant and ironic. For the woman, there is the Feminist demanding her rights. She insists on being regarded not merely as dependent woman but on playing an independent role in love and impressing men as capable of being detached and analytical—as having a "man's attitude." And for the mystic, there is the agnostic, the self-conscious modern, who is much aware of being cut off from traditional religion and standing alone in the midst of the indifferent universe that Hardy and Housman presented.

Thus, one might interpret Millay as a person who combined a teasing boy, an indignant satirist, a schoolmarmish Feminist, and a tough-minded agnostic. Yet she is also all the things DuBois mentioned. From these paradoxes, one supposes, come Millay's variety and her elusiveness stressed by Miriam Gurko, the attitude of gallantry-in-the-midst-of-tears, and the frequent irony in her writing. Hers is a classic case of the romantic irony found in Heinrich Heine and in other romantic poets. She has been compared to Byron; certainly, like him, she was an unusual combination of heart and head; she was romantic at heart but had respect for classic poetry and a strong tendency toward satire.

Millay earned a reputation as one of the leading poets of her time. Being a woman, she wrote with a great sensitivity about personal relationships and about the condition of the world. Her attitudes, especially those regarding love and the situation of women, exemplified those of the twentieth century; but she was more than a woman poet. She was a modern humanist and a radical; her humanism and her radicalism were immutable qualities. She was typical of the World War I generation that gave the 1920's their characteristic tone, but much of her writing transcends the 1920's.

Her reputation suffered because of her propaganda poems of World War II, and with changing fashions she has been cast into a limbo of critical neglect. It is time for a reconsideration of her work; toward this objective the present study is directed. When John Patton's projected bibliography, *A Comprehensive Bibliography of Millay Criticism*, is published and when there is a Millay concordance and a thorough study of her versification, critical assessment of Millay can be completed. Meanwhile, this is the first study to discuss in some detail almost the whole range of her writing.

Preface

It has not been possible, of course, to discuss every item that Millay wrote. Her "Nancy Boyd" stories and her prose sketches have not been considered, and for lack of space many of her poems have not been mentioned. An attempt has been made, however, to consider all the major works and to examine a sufficient number of the less important ones to illustrate the poet's attitudes, her favorite topics, and her poetic development.

Following the chronology and the chapters containing the account of her life, Millay's works are treated in a prevailingly chronological order. Chapter IV takes up her first three books of lyrics. In Chapter V her dramatic works are discussed. Chapter VI is devoted to the work of her maturity through *Flowers of Evil* (1936), and Chapter VII considers the poetry from *Conversation at Midnight* through the posthumous collections. Chapter VIII supplies a brief record of the critical reception of Millay's work and an estimate of her achievement.

In writing this book I received help from every person of whom I asked it. My thanks are due especially to Norma Millay and to her husband, Charles Ellis, for their inspiriting assistance and hospitality at Steepletop. I gratefully acknowledge that I also owe much to Witter Bynner; Clarence R. Decker; Floyd Dell, for conversations and letters; George Dillon, for a generous letter explaining his work with Millay on *Flowers of Evil*; Harrison Dowd; Mrs. Arthur Davison Ficke, for permission to consult material in the Arthur Davison Ficke Collection in the Yale University Library; Miriam Gurko, for a long evening's conversation that seemed short, at a time inconvenient for her; Mrs. Beulah Hagen of Harper and Row, Publishers; Muna Lee; John Patton; and Edmund Wilson. I am also grateful for help received from Donald Gallup, Curator of American Literature, Yale University Library; Miss Dorothy A. Plum, Bibliographer, and Miss Jean McFarland, Librarian, of the Vassar College Library; and members of the library staffs of Auburn University, New York University, the University of Puerto Rico, and the New York Public Library.

NORMAN A. BRITTIN

University of Puerto Rico
April, 1966

Acknowledgments

For the use of certain materials, I am grateful to the following:

Norma Millay for permission to quote from the following sources published by Harper and Brothers: *Collected Poems*, copyright 1917, 1921, 1922, 1923, 1928, 1931, 1933, 1934, 1936, 1937, 1938, 1939, 1940, 1941, 1950 by Edna St. Vincent Millay; copyright 1945, 1946, 1951, 1952, 1953, 1954, 1956 by Norma Millay Ellis. *Three Plays*, copyright 1926 by Edna St. Vincent Millay; copyright 1953 by Norma Millay Ellis. *The King's Henchman*, copyright 1927 by Edna St. Vincent Millay; copyright 1954 by Norma Millay Ellis. *The Princess Marries the Page*, copyright 1932 by Edna St. Vincent Millay; copyright 1960 by Norma Millay Ellis. *Flowers of Evil*, copyright 1936 by George Dillon and Edna St. Vincent Millay; copyright 1963 by Norma Millay Ellis and George Dillon. *Conversation at Midnight*, copyright 1937 by Edna St. Vincent Millay; copyright 1964 by Norma Millay Ellis. *Huntsman, What Quarry?*, copyright 1939 by Edna St. Vincent Millay. *Make Bright the Arrows*, copyright 1940 by Edna St. Vincent Millay. *The Murder of Lidice*, copyright 1942 by Edna St. Vincent Millay. *Distressing Dialogues*, copyright 1924 by Edna St. Vincent Millay; copyright 1951 by Norma Millay Ellis. *Letters of Edna St. Vincent Millay*, copyright 1952 by Norma Millay Ellis.

Edmund Wilson for permission to quote his poem "Provincetown" from "Epilogue, 1952: Edna St. Vincent Millay," in *The Shores of Light*, published 1952 by Farrar, Straus and Young, Inc.

Alfred A. Knopf, Incorporated, for permission to quote from *Selected Poems* by Arthur Davison Ficke.

The Yale University Library for permission to publish information from the Arthur Davison Ficke Collection and other material by and about Edna St. Vincent Millay.

Contents

Chronology

1892   Edna St. Vincent Millay born February 22 at Rockland, Maine; first child of Henry Tolman Millay and Cora Buzzelle Millay, who encouraged her daughter to excel in music and poetry.

1900   Parents divorced.

1905-   Attended high school in Camden, Maine; became editor-
1909   in-chief of school magazine.

1906-   Poems published by *St. Nicholas Magazine.*
1910

1912   Attracted attention of Caroline B. Dow, who enabled her to enroll in college. Attracted national attention for "Renascence" upon publication of *The Lyric Year* in November.

1913   Attended Barnard College to prepare for entrance to Vassar College, which she entered in autumn.

1915-   Played in Vassar productions of several plays; wrote and
1917   took the leading part in *The Princess Marries the Page*; graduated with A.B., 1917.

1917   *Renascence and Other Poems.* To New York in the fall; acted with Provincetown Players.

1918   Lived in poverty in Greenwich Village while acting. Love affairs with Floyd Dell, Arthur Davison Ficke, and others.

1919   Poems (and stories under pseudonym Nancy Boyd) in *Ainslee's.* Finished *Aria da Capo* and directed it for Provincetown Players; first performance, December 5.

1920   Publications in *Vanity Fair* and *Reedy's Mirror.* Received $100 prize from *Poetry* for "The Bean-Stalk." *A Few Figs from Thistles* and *Aria da Capo.* Left for Europe to write for *Vanity Fair.*

1921   European travel. *Two Slatterns and a King, The Lamp and the Bell,* and *Second April.*

1922 With $500 advance on *Hardigut,* a novel, brought her mother to Europe. Health poor.

1923 February, returned to the United States. Received Pulitzer Prize for poetry. Serious illness. Married Eugen Jan Boissevain, July 18. *The Harp-Weaver and Other Poems.*

1924 January, began reading tours. With husband, toured Orient. *Distressing Dialogues* (by Nancy Boyd).

1925 Reading tours. June 15, honorary Litt.D. degree from Tufts College. She and husband bought farm (Steepletop) at Austerlitz, New York; their home for the rest of their lives.

1927 February 17, Metropolitan Opera premiere of *The King's Henchman.* August, participated in Boston protests against execution of Sacco and Vanzetti.

1928 *The Buck in the Snow.* Ten sonnets of "Epitaph for the Race of Man" in St. Louis *Post-Dispatch* (December).

1929 Elected to National Institute of Arts and Letters; *Poems Selected for Young People.*

1931 *Fatal Interview.* Received Helen Haire Levinson Prize for sonnets in *Poetry* (October, 1930).

1932 *The Princess Marries the Page.* December 25, first of a series of eight national radio broadcasts on which she very successfully read her poems.

1933 February 2, presented Prix Femina to Willa Cather. May 22, Laureate of General Federation of Women's Clubs. Litt.D. degrees from University of Wisconsin and Russell Sage College.

1934 November 1, *Wine from These Grapes.*

1935 Summer, worked with George Dillon on Baudelaire translation.

1936 April, *Flowers of Evil* (with George Dillon). May 2, manuscript of *Conversation at Midnight* destroyed in hotel fire, Sanibel Island, Florida. Summer, injury to nerves of back. December-May, 1937, in New York rewriting *Conversation at Midnight.*

1937   June, honorary L.H.D. from New York University, honorary Litt.D. from Colby College. *Conversation at Midnight.*

1939   Intense interest in international situation.

1940   May, began writing propaganda. November, elected to American Academy of Arts and Letters. *Make Bright the Arrows.*

1941   Recorded her poems for RCA Victor. *Collected Sonnets.*

1942   *The Murder of Lidice.*

1943   January 31, received Gold Medal of the Poetry Society of America.

1944   Summer, nervous breakdown; unable to write for two years.

1949   August 30, Eugen Jan Boissevain died in Boston of a stroke after an operation. After hospitalization, she returned to live alone at Steepletop.

1950   While living alone in great grief, continued writing until her death of heart failure on October 19.

1952   *Letters of Edna St. Vincent Millay.*

1954   *Mine the Harvest.*

1956   *Collected Poems.*

Edna St. Vincent Millay

CHAPTER 1

'These Were the Things
That Bounded Me'

C ARRYING a pail of blueberries she had just picked in the pastures outside Camden, Maine, Edna St. Vincent Millay, a tiny red-headed girl of twenty, approached her home in the town and saw her mother waiting on the doorstep with a letter in her hand. The letter, addressed to "E. Vincent Millay, Esq.," was from Ferdinand Earle, sponsor of *The Lyric Year*. It expressed his enthusiasm over a poem entitled "Renaissance" and—prematurely—his confidence that the poem would be awarded the five-hundred-dollar first prize in the *Lyric Year* contest. This vivid little episode brought together at that moment of 1912 three of the essential elements of Edna St. Vincent Millay's poetic career. These were the precocious talent of the young woman; the Maine background of pasture, mountain, and seashore; and the strong and inspiring figure of the poet's mother, Cora Millay.

I *"The Courage That My Mother Had"*

Mrs. Millay was a woman of musical talent who had been a singer. She was a woman independent enough to separate from her husband, the charming—perhaps brilliant, but undependable—poker-playing Henry Tolman Millay. She was tough enough to earn a living for herself and her three daughters; and she was so zealous for her children's development that, even though they may have lacked creature comforts at times, she saw to it that they had books, music lessons, and incentive to express themselves and to excel. The three girls were all quick-minded, imaginative, and responsive to the opportunities that their mother (with an occasional gift from the father) could provide them in a small resort and mill town. Of the three, Vincent, the eldest—apparently she was never called Edna by the family—at an early age revealed extraordinary capabilities.

With a minimum of rancor, Mrs. Millay had divorced her husband about 1900 and settled in Camden. Before, the family had lived in several small towns of northeastern Massachusetts and the Penobscot region, where Henry Millay had been a school principal and superintendent. Mrs. Millay was of old New England stock that had first settled in Ipswich, Massachusetts, in 1634.[1] Strains of Irish blood in their ancestry may have been responsible for the imaginative energy of the three girls.

On the other hand, New England respect for education, New England self-reliance and composure in the face of poverty were important parts of the home environment in which Vincent and her sisters were reared. Since nursing often kept the mother away from home at mealtimes and at night, the girls, under Vincent's leadership, became self-reliant. Constant work and invigorating study were almost like play. Dishwashing was relatively painless as they sang Vincent's composition "I'm the Queen of the Dishpans."[2] It was more important to read, write, sing, and learn than to become slaves to dusting, mopping, mending, and cooking.

Mrs. Millay had taught Vincent the elements of music. John Tufts, a retired music teacher who heard the young girl play her own composition in 1905, volunteered to give her piano lessons. For some three years she studied with him to become a concert pianist, but he finally decided that her hands were too tiny to allow her to fulfill such an ambition.[3] Whatever her disappointment, she acquired a considerable amount of musical knowledge and skill, which were to aid her in her career.

Vincent skipped the eighth grade and at the age of thirteen was "The Newest Freshman" in the Camden High School. She wrote a composition with that title, and it was published in the high school magazine. She mentioned her excitement while reading a criticism of Darwin's theory.[4] Probably not many Maine girls of thirteen were stimulated by such criticisms. Norma Millay, Vincent's younger sister, attributes this interest in scientific matters to the circumstance that their mother, who had the best private library in town, gave her daughters constant encouragement to read books and magazines.

II *"Tall Elms, My Roots Go Down"*

In 1902, when Vincent was in the fourth grade, she had sub-
scribed to *Harper's Young People*; and in 1905 she had joined the
St. Nicholas League (for aspiring writers under eighteen) of *St.
Nicholas Magazine*. *St. Nicholas* accepted "Forest Trees," her first
poem to be published (October, 1906). The third stanza of the
poem, like the sestet of an Italian sonnet, reveals an awareness of
geologic processes and an imaginative concept of the vast reaches
of time through which the forest persists:

> Around you all is change—where now is land
> Swift vessels plowed to foam the seething main;
> Kingdoms have risen, and the fire fiend's hand
> Has crushed them to their mother earth again;
> And through it all ye stand, and still will stand
> Till ages yet to come have owned your reign.

The stanza is reminiscent of Tennyson's *In Memoriam* (Section
123): "There rolls the deep where grew the tree./O earth, what
changes hast thou seen!" It is also prophetic of "Epitaph for the
Race of Man."

Vincent was on the staff of the high school magazine and became editor-in-chief in her senior year. *St. Nicholas* published five
other poems—one of which, "The Land of Romance," received the
Gold Badge of the St. Nicholas League. Yet the boys of her class,
acting in collusion, elected a boy Class Poet. Vincent showed her
mettle, however, by reciting as her senior essay at the graduation
exercises a poem, "Le Joie de Vivre."[5] For the essay she received
a prize of ten dollars.

"The Land of Romance" was reprinted in *Current Literature*
(April, 1907) along with E. A. Robinson's "Miniver Cheevy" and
work by Thomas Bailey Aldrich, Edwin Markham, and Witter
Bynner. It was thought a remarkable production for a fourteen-
year-old. In the summer of 1910 she received a prize of five dollars for "Friends." She said she would use the money to buy "a
beautiful copy of 'Browning,' whom I admire so much. . . ." Actually, "Friends," a pair of contrasting soliloquies, is a bit like
Browning. In "The Land of Romance" one may detect the influ-

ence of Poe and the decadent poets of the 1890's. The poem has many trite, romantic tags and closes with "The breath of dying lilies haunted the twilight air,/And the sob of a dreaming violin filled the silence everywhere." The juvenilia of Millay are, in general, romantic—rather Tennysonian—and show her interest in using various meters.

In the summer of 1907 Vincent had worked as a typist; in her leisure she had written her first sonnet, "Old Letters."[6] After graduation she took occasional jobs, usually as a stenographer for summer visitors.[7] She had taken part in class plays in high school, and after high school she did some acting in amateur theatricals and with stock companies traveling through.[8] She participated in the usual girls' activities of a small seaside town; and, while her mother was away in the summer of 1911, she did most of the cooking at home while also writing poems.

Her poetry was improving and exhibiting more human concern; but though she submitted it to many editors, none of it was published. Only her mother, sisters, and a few other townspeople were aware of her writing. One would imagine that Vincent felt uncertainty and possibly creative frustration as she walked down the streets to the chatter of looms in the woolen mills; as she swam in the river; as she climbed steep Mount Battie, an eight-hundred-foot spur just behind the town; or as she rambled about the pastures and hills along the three-mile road to Lake Megunticook with its beautiful irregular shoreline.[9]

At least she had the advantage—as did Wordsworth—of a daily life "incorporated with the beautiful and permanent forms of nature."[10] Gorham Munson compares the Penobscot country to the English Lake District and calls it "ideal Poet's country."[11] Views of mountains, woods, fields, sea, and coastline became indelibly impressed upon an adolescent heart. The waves, the winds whirling spray over rocks and wharves, the seaweed and green piles, the gulls tacking into the breeze—there was no item of this coastal life that she did not remember. Like many another writer, she could never free herself of the hold which nature in this one particular place had upon her; and she never wished to. When she was past forty, she wrote of the Penobscot country as her *pays,* like that part of the world a Frenchman really loves, "bounded only by the horizon of his early associations. . . ."[12]

III   "The First . . . To Think My Poetry of Some Consequence"

Scarcely had Vincent passed her twentieth birthday when news came in late February, 1912, that her father was seriously ill. She traveled to Kingman, Maine, a village a hundred miles north where Henry Millay was then living. While her father recovered, she stayed with his physician, Dr. Somerville, who with his daughter did all he could to make her stay pleasant. During this interlude an important announcement arrived. In a house where she was attending a case, Mrs. Millay had picked up a discarded magazine that contained news of the proposed annual anthology *The Lyric Year*; and she suggested that her daughter come home and submit something for the contest. Vincent completed "Renaissance" and sent it in, along with a dramatic soliloquy in blank verse entitled "Interim."

Slogging through the ten thousand entries received ("piles of disgustingly awful *rot* that was submitted to me as poetry"),[13] Ferdinand Earle rejoiced when he read "Renaissance." Even so, the extreme simplicity of its opening lines almost caused it to be discarded by Professor Donner, a friend helping sift manuscripts. After reading the poem twice, both Donner and Earle "agreed that it was tops." Not taking into account the other two judges, Earle rushed off the over-hasty announcement of success which must have kindled in Vincent and in the other Millays exuberant joy and tingling satisfaction.

Considerable correspondence followed between Vincent and Earle, during which she accepted his proposal that the title of her poem be changed to "Renascence." He also became convinced of her gender and informed Arthur Davison Ficke a few months later:

> . . . I wrote to "Mr. E. Vincent Millay" to express my amazement at the beauty of his piece. Imagine my feelings at receiving the photo of a mite of a girl, and a saucy letter of thanks.
> It is only after months of correspondence and inquiry that I am convinced that the author is really Miss Twenty Years, saucier and more attractive than ever, tho' poor as a church mouse and living in a little village in Maine. She is to be sent next fall to Vassar by some well-to-do friends.[14]

The promise of success—fame and money—had been tempered by disappointment. Earle's fellow judges were William Stanley Braithwaite, poetry editor of the Boston *Transcript*, and Edward J. Wheeler, editor of *Current Opinion* and president of the Poetry Society of America. Wheeler favored the poetry of "social consciousness," stemming from Whitman and exemplified at the turn of the century by the work of Edwin Markham and William Vaughn Moody. So in spite of Earle's efforts to bring the other judges to his thinking about "Renascence," when the votes were cast, the first prize went to Orrick Johns for "Second Avenue," the second to Thomas Augustine Daly for "To a Thrush," and the third to George Sterling for "An Ode for the Centenary of the Birth of Robert Browning." The last two poems were distinctly Victorian and lacking in "social content."[15]

"Renascence" received Earle's vote for first place but no other votes, and so it was given fourth place and no prize. Earle's enthusiasm for "Renascence" was a unique tribute to poetic quality, for he wrote in a "Note by the Editor" in *The Lyric Year* that he had "endeavored to give preference to poems fired with the Time Spirit. . . . Our twentieth century poetry is democratic, scientific, humane. Its independence reveals the liberating touch of Walt Whitman, sweet with robust optimism."

When *The Lyric Year* was published in November, 1912, "Renascence" received great critical acclaim, and the judges were blamed for failing to recognize its excellence. Orrick Johns himself felt that he had received "an unmerited award"; Louis Untermeyer praised "Renascence" in the Chicago *Post*; and both Arthur Davison Ficke and Witter Bynner, whose poems also appeared in *The Lyric Year*, wrote appreciatively to the unknown Maine author.

Toward the end of the summer "Renascence" had produced another explosion of interest which led to decisions and actions that greatly influenced the poet's future. In the course of an evening party at the Whitehall Inn in Camden, Vincent was prevailed upon to play the piano, sing, and recite. One of the summer visitors was impelled to action by hearing "Renascence." This was Miss Caroline B. Dow, head of the National Training School of the YWCA in New York City. Discovering that Vincent had composed the songs and the poem—and that it was to be published in

The Lyric Year—Miss Dow suggested that Vincent apply for a scholarship at Smith or Vassar. She promised that money for other expenses would be provided.

In early January, 1913, Vincent informed her mother that girls from the Orient but very few from Maine were enrolled in Vassar —so she preferred to go there. She had sent poems to the Poetry Society of America and also to Ficke, whose opinion she thought would be adverse. She told him: "It is quite true that I have yet to learn the ABC's of my art. I am hoping that college will help me;—but if I should come back a suffragette instead of a poet wouldn't it be dreadful?" Evidently she was not prepared at this point to consider that she might develop as both suffragette and poet. Vassar was to be her college, but in order to meet requirements for entrance she had to make up courses.

When Miss Dow had inquired in October about her reading, Vincent had sent her a list which, she said, "must seem awfully crazy to you. I've really read so much that I hardly know what to pick out." She set down Shakespeare, Dickens, Eliot, Scott, Tennyson, Milton, and Wordsworth as authors with whom she was "very well acquainted"; but she felt well acquainted with Hawthorne, Browning, Kipling, Barrie, Mark Twain, and Elbert Hubbard. She listed also some thirty works, mostly novels, of which a dozen were classics. She was an ardent reader, and the quality of her list speaks well for the solid preparation she had had at home and in Camden High School. She tended to speak disparagingly of her knowledge of history and mathematics;[16] her main interest lay in literature and in Latin and French.

IV *"You Can Get Accustomed to Anything"*

In early February, 1913, she left Camden for the metropolis, a country mouse eager for new experiences in the great world of New York City where she attended Barnard College for one semester. Vincent responded to New York with zest and irony. On February 5, 1913, she reported to Arthur Ficke: "And the view— charming, charming! So many roofs and things, you know; warships, and chimneys, and brewery signs—so inspiring!" High spirits, a twinkling eye, and a mock-heroic manner are evident in her letters of this time.

She was gratified by being included in activities of the Poetry Society, by an early invitation to have tea with Sara Teasdale, and by a literary evening given expressly for her on March 9 by Jessie B. Rittenhouse, Secretary of the Poetry Society. All, wrote Miss Rittenhouse, "were on the *qui vive* to meet her. Pretty, petite, not yet over the wonder of her sudden entry upon the literary scene, she was altogether natural and charming."[17]

To be in New York then—she had attended the famous Armory Show the day before the Rittenhouse party—and to meet literary lions on equal terms must have been a heady experience. Though she wrote Ficke that she was settled down like a wheel in a rut, she said, "Sometimes . . . I feel that I am exceeding the speed-limit." She had a sense of triumph from selling "Journey" and "God's World" to Mitchell Kennerley, publisher of *The Lyric Year*; he soon issued them in *The Forum*. The twenty-five-dollar check was a heartening pledge of future success: "It seems as if this had broken my hoodoo of 'all praise and no profit.'" Inclined to be apologetic about "Journey," she informed her family: "It isn't anything great, I know. But Miss Rittenhouse says it is nothing I need be ashamed of even if it does come after *Renascence*. . . ." Could she live up to the reputation "Renascence" had brought her? This question must have haunted her a bit, and therefore Kennerley's check must have been doubly reassuring.

As for her work at Barnard, Vincent's letters make one aware only of a writing course taught by William Tenney Brewster; in it she was very successful. He called her poem "Interim" "a very remarkable production for a girl in college" and praised her story "Barbara on the Beach." A student in the class wanted the story for the college magazine; but Vincent, evidently thinking that she could sell it, refused her. The story was printed in the *Smart Set* for November, 1914.

Her many activities kept her extraordinarily busy; small wonder that she told her family, "I've too much to do to bother with men." Nevertheless, she was escorted about the city on occasion by Salomón de la Selva, a young poet from Nicaragua. With him she rode on the old double-decker buses and took the five-cent ferry ride to Staten Island where couples could have picnics, swim at some beach, walk through the woods, or even lie "on a hill-top underneath the moon," as she writes in "Recuerdo." Such a ferry ride with De la Selva was evidently the occasion for "Recuerdo," the Spanish title delicately complimenting her companion, who was becoming her admirer.[18]

After returning to Camden when the semester was over, she wrote Ficke on July 8 that "Latin Prose all summer" was the first order of business; she was being tutored for the "stiff entrance examination in Latin writing"[19] through correspondence with a Vassar Latin professor, Elizabeth Hazelton Haight, who became her lifelong friend. Having accepted Ficke more or less as her mentor during the previous winter, she wrote him in January: "I imagine it will be some time yet before I get right up and 'speak in meetin'.' . . . I have gratefully absorbed into my system all you said. . . ." But she was independent, and her correspondence with her "Dear Spiritual Advisor" did not become too serious; the Roman candles of her pertness constantly jet their colors over her letters. Ficke, man of charm and wit that he was, elicited unstodgy responses.

V *"This Pink-and-Gray College"*

Vincent was admitted to Vassar College with the Class of 1917. Though by no means old, the College had an excellent faculty and a dynamic spirit. Henry Noble MacCracken, who became its president in December, 1914, "was amazed to find the quality of teaching at Vassar better" than that he had known at Harvard and Yale.[20] But the first response of Vincent, then twenty-one, was hostile. She revealed her feelings to Ficke:

> I hate this pink-and-gray college. If there had been a college in *Alice-in-Wonderland* it would be this college. Every morning when I awake I swear, I say, "Damn this pink-and-gray college!" . . .
> They treat us like an orphan asylum. . . .
> They trust us with everything but men,—and they let us see it, so that it's worse than not trusting us at all. We can go into the candy-kitchen and take what we like and pay or not and nobody is there to know. But a man is forbidden as if he were an apple.

Her maturity, her independence, and her idealism were affronted by the strictness of college rules; but she did not long retain this attitude of flaming negation. The courses and other activities soon elicited her loyal and excellent efforts.

During the summer of 1914 "Interim" was published in the Vassar *Miscellany* for July and in the September *Forum*. By the end of her sophomore year she had established herself not only as a writer but also as an actress. Each year she played two or more progressively better roles.[21] For Founder's Day in May, 1915, she prepared the words for the class Marching Song; and on May 21 she wrote her mother that she had been given the part of Marie de France in the pageant being prepared to celebrate Vassar's fiftieth anniversary the next fall.

President MacCracken called the 1890-1915 era at Vassar the period of the crusader.[22] A Socialist Club and a Suffrage Club were founded in 1915.[23] When Inez Milholland, a graduate of 1909, who had become a lawyer and suffragette leader also "active in New York shirtwaist and laundry strikes," appeared at the fiftieth anniversary, she was, MacCracken said, "clearly the idol of the undergraduates."[24] This Amazon, famous for her "brilliant, large-featured beauty,"[25] was an immensely magnetic young woman; in private life she was the wife of Eugen Boissevain, a Dutchman to whom she was married in 1913. She gave Vincent her most dramatic example of feminism in action.

The Vassar students, who had worked two years on the script of the Pageant of Athena, "a cooperative story of women's intellectual advancement,"[26] presented it on October 11, 1915, as part of the great anniversary celebration. When Vincent's scene came that afternoon and strings played a *gigue*, she entered "shyly but eagerly," as the medieval French poet Marie de France; two pages carried the train of her white satin and silver costume; and her long, auburn hair was adorned with pearls.[27] Her recitation of the *lai* of the Honeysuckle, a story of Tristram and Iseult, "greatly moved the audience." MacCracken thought her scene "was perhaps the loveliest of all the many scenes" of the pageant.[28] Vassar authorities were criticized, however, "for allowing students in the pageant to dance in bare feet and legs."[29]

No less busy at Vassar than she had been in Camden and in New York, Vincent filled her college years with rewarding work, both creative and academic. Her courses were chiefly in literature and languages. She studied not only Latin and French but also Greek, Italian, Spanish, and German. In addition to an advanced writing course and a course in Techniques of the Drama, she took courses in Nineteenth Century Poetry, History of the Drama, Chaucer, and Old English. Professor Haight treated her as an equal, and Vincent owed to her a deep and permanent interest in Latin poetry. Although Vincent shared the tremendous Vassar interest in drama and singing, she acquired with her courses a foundation of sound literary knowledge. Her education reinforced the influence of the classics upon her and insured that she would be a learned poet, one more like a Milton, Shelley, or Tennyson than a Whitman or Vachel Lindsay.

In her senior year Vincent brought her dramatic career at Vassar to its climax with the lead role in *The Princess Marries the Page*, which she herself had written. Another play of hers, *The Wall of Dominoes*, was published in the *Vassar Miscellany* for May, 1917. Her achievements as an actress gave her the idea of seeking a career on the stage. She had kept in touch with Salomón de la Selva, who introduced her to Ralph Roeder, a member of the Washington Square Players. She was busy thinking ahead: having already arranged for her youngest sister, Kathleen, to enter Vassar, Vincent suggested that as soon as she had a good job in New York, Norma must come there to study at the School of Design: "You're the most talented one of us all, & you've got to have your chance, too. Of course Mother must come & we'd just leave Camden forever, I suppose. . . ."

She had other contacts with the world outside Vassar. John Masefield wrote her; and in early December, 1916, she sold three poems to Harriet Monroe's *Poetry*. On January 27, 1917, she wrote a gay letter to Sara Teasdale, who had recently been married to Ernst Filsinger, giving her permission to reprint "Ashes of Life" in *The Answering Voice*, an anthology of love poetry by women: "Whadda you mean by having husbands and anthologys at the same time like that *Vile Inseck the Emancipated Woman*?. . . ."[30]

She had expressed what no doubt generations of Vassar students felt in a piece printed in the *Vassar Miscellany Monthly*, "Why Did I Ever Come to This Place? (An expedition in untrammelled verse)," which has as refrain "woman's place/Is in the home." Such tongue-in-cheek doubt about that "*Vile Inseck the Emancipated Woman*" was, however, inconsistent with the confident mood with which she viewed the future. Graduation itself was unfortunately snarled up because of certain Vassar regulations, innocently broken. Vincent was rusticated from the campus, and there was a hot controversy. She reported home that it seemed "pretty shabby, . . . after all that I have done for the college"; but she was nevertheless elated over the "wonderful news, maybe," that she might be able to act in Milwaukee for eight weeks that summer with Edith Wynne Matthison. Finally, she was able to write in triumph: ". . . I graduated in my cap & gown along with the rest. . . . Commencement went off beautifully . . . (Edna St. Vincent Millay A.B.!)."

CHAPTER 2

'I Am Not a Tentative Person'

VINCENT spent the summer of 1917 at home since she had not been hired for the Milwaukee season. From actress Edith Wynne Matthison (Mrs. Charles Rann Kennedy) she had received letters of recommendation, and she wrote Mrs. Kennedy in a tone of rather self-conscious gracious formality. Her independence is revealed in a number of passages:

> Listen; if ever in my letters to you, or in my conversation, you see a candor that seems almost crude,—please know that it is because when I think of you I think of real things, & become honest, —and quibbling and circumvention seem very inconsiderable.

. . . .

> Love me, please; I love you; I can bear to be your friend. So ask of me anything, and hurt me whenever you must; but never be "tolerant," or "kind." And never say to me again,—don't dare to say to me again—"Anyway, you can make a trial" of being friends with you! Because I can't do things in that way; I am not a tentative person. Whatever I do, I give my whole self up to it. . . . Didn't you just say that to frighten me into consciousness of the enormity of being friends with you?—But enormity does not frighten me; it is only among tremendous things that I feel happy and at ease; I would not say this, perhaps, except that, as I told you, I do not trouble to lie to you.

I   "Blossom Time Is Early, But No Fruit Sets On"

In early September Vincent visited the Kennedys in Connecticut. Impressed by her poetry, they arranged some readings for her. She hopefully typed a collection of her poems for Mitchell Kennerley, who had persuaded her to let him publish it; she thought it would sell well for Christmas presents. Then she went to New York. She was too jealous of her independence to become a secretary to a wealthy woman or to take a position as a governess. She had interviews with theatrical managers and began to give public readings of her poetry. Though she had failed to obtain a job in the theater, she had fifty dollars for a week of readings and coaching productions or her own *Two Slatterns and a King* and *The Princess Marries the Page* at the Bennet School. Her correspondence reveals a bold, adventurous spirit. She was again much stimulated by New York, where she was going about with Salomón de la Selva.

That fall Kennerley published her first collection, *Renascence and Other Poems*; but she received no money from it. She and Norma had decided, however, that Norma was to join her in New York. Vincent told her sister that it would be hard for them; but, she said, "We're bound to succeed—can't keep us down—I'm all enthusiasm and good courage about it." Shortly, indeed, Vincent made a connection with the theater which proved to be of importance in the development of her career. Hearing that an actress was needed by the Provincetown Players, she read for the ingénue part in Floyd Dell's *The Angel Intrudes* and secured it—but at no salary since the Provincetown group was unable to pay its performers.[1] The play opened December 28, 1917, in the Playwrights' Theatre at 139 Macdougal Street, deep in Greenwich Village, during some of New York's coldest weather. Pleased with the way his new actress took direction and with her performance, Dell offered her a part in his next play, *Sweet and Twenty*, which she accepted.[2] It seemed best then for the Millay sisters to live in the Village (Norma worked in a loft, checking thread-gauge wires used on airplanes),[3] where rents were cheap; and in January, 1918, the sisters moved from the National Training School to West Ninth Street and soon after to Waverly Place.

Thus Vincent was brought into contact with some of the most brilliant and vigorous personalities of the time in a *milieu* where advanced ideas were common coin. The Village was congenial to her, and she had opportunities there that she could have had nowhere else. At one time a separate community, Greenwich Village had been engulfed by spreading New York. Yet the gigantic beanstalk growth of the metropolis had left half-unfolded, one might say, a single leaf still crumpled, still tender and untoughened by the brassy sun of commerce that beat so hotly uptown. A particular kind of Bohemian life developed among the crooked streets lined by old red-brick houses which, decades earlier, had been fashionable.[4] By the beginning of the twentieth century this decayed area had a picturesqueness not to be found elsewhere in New York. The cheap rents attracted poor but ambitious artists and writers; picturesqueness pleased them; and the spirit of the *milieu* enticed them often to become permanent dwellers in "this island paradise . . . safe out of change's way."[5]

The spirit was, in a sense, that of a village: here was a small definite area where human beings could live simply, not overwhelmed by hugeness, rush, noise, and anonymity. The Villagers saw each other frequently in a casual, natural way as they bought groceries and cheap wine, crossed Macdougal Street or Greenwich Avenue, strolled through Washington Square, or dropped in at restaurants, bookstores, playhouses, and saloons that were as accessible as they would have been in any small town. But in a more significant sense the spirit of Greenwich Village was quite unlike that of the usual American village; in fact, this very difference drew young men and women to the Village and made them vehement defenders of its values. The Villagers asserted that the great touchstone of the Village spirit was honesty. In the Village a person could be himself. He did not have to give "forc't Halleluiah's" to Wall Street, Main Street, the government, or Mrs. Grundy. He was not obliged to drink behind the barn because Aunt Susie wielded the gavel for the WCTU or to appear in church because it would look bad for his family if he did not. He was not obliged to disguise his interest in art or poetry, to go hungry for discussion of it, or to conceal his boredom with prevailing American taste and American politics. The unconventionality so conspicuous to visitors was an expression of an honest individualism that many Americans had always considered the heart of the American tradition.

One might say that people came to Greenwich Village because there, as in few other places, they could be Bohemian; they could be free of the dominant middle-class values. In a way, Greenwich Village was the urban obverse of Brook Farm, another attempt to gratify the artist's "utopian wish."[6]

When Millay went there, the Village was characterized by its attractive spirit of individualism, of integrity at all costs. For the many inhabitants who made names for themselves, the basic Village honesty accompanied hard work, gay camaraderie, vigorous play which sometimes went to wildness, and a fierce intensification of the sense of life. Malcolm Cowley wrote: "It didn't matter that we were penniless: . . . we were continually drunk with high spirits."[7]

It would be incorrect to say that Greenwich Village converted Millay to *avant-garde* ways, to Feminism, free thinking, Bohemianism, or political radicalism. Both Witter Bynner and Floyd Dell believe that she would not have been an essentially different person had she never come to the Village.[8] She was nearly twenty-six years old when she went there to live, and she knew what she stood for. Nevertheless, the contact with young, vigorous, and radical minds in the bubbling libertarian pot of the Village provided a kind of corroboration—a strengthening into ultimate conviction, through agreement and contention—of the values that she believed in. Village directness and disdain of hypocrisy would be congenial to one who was not a tentative person and who scorned quibbling and circumvention. The Greenwich Villagers were her friends; and though she was too intent upon her work to waste time with Bohemian frauds, she was engaged in activities characteristic of the Village.

She came at times to the Liberal Club; she knew contributors to the *Masses* and to the *Liberator*; she was a member of the Provincetown Players and a friendly ally of the Washington Square group; and she felt all the warm, generous, youthful, idealistic or disillusioning gusts of feeling that blew through the Village during the war and post-war years. As far as habitat was concerned, she was not a confirmed Villager; but there were few issues on which her stand from 1917 to 1929 would have been distinguishable from that of the Village.

The long list of those whom Millay encountered in the Village would constitute a roll of honor in contemporary American arts and letters: Max Eastman, Floyd Dell, Mary Heaton Vorse, John Reed, Emmanuel Carnevali, Alfred Kreymborg, Theodore Dreiser, Malcolm Cowley, Kenneth Burke, Frank Shay, Phyllis

Duganne, Harry Kemp, Dorothy Day, Hutchins Hapgood, Paul Robeson, Arthur Garfield Hays, E. E. Cummings, Hart Crane, Llewelyn Powys, Pieter Mijer, John Sloan, the Zorachs, Wallace Stevens, Edmund Wilson, and John Peale Bishop. She also knew such "village figures" as Romany Marie and Bobby Edwards; those particularly interested in the art theater, such as George Cram Cook and Susan Glaspell, Robert Edmond Jones, Rita Wellman, Eugene O'Neill, and Djuna Barnes; Lawrence Langner, Rollo Peters, and other founders of The Theatre Guild. And some who, though not actually Villagers, were sympathetic visitors, such as Louis Untermeyer, William Carlos Williams, and Harold Loeb.

A number of these people were political radicals. Max Eastman had become editor of the Socialist *Masses* in 1912; and Dell, soon after arriving from Chicago in 1913, had joined him as associate editor. John Reed was drawn to radicalism when reporting the Paterson silk workers' strike and the Ludlow miners' strike in 1913. Mary Heaton Vorse, of an old New England family, had also taken the strikers' side in various disputes. Millay's views generally chimed with theirs.

The Provincetown Players, headed by George Cram Cook, had a playwrights' theater. They wished to give writers a chance to create new plays *and to see them produced.*[9] Some of the members wrote plays, mostly one-acters. Other members were expected to pay dues, to assist with production, and even to act in the plays, however lacking in professional experience they might be. Their plays represented a radical venture—a challenge to the commercial theater that at first was hardly recognized: "Radicalism at the moment meant deeper realism than Broadway audiences were ready to face. . . . Here was native insurgency at its best: a theater that did more than any other to open the channel of creative play writing. A theater that staged its offerings only passably well, sometimes very crudely, but never with the false glamour of typical Broadway staging."[10]

Floyd Dell's plays are all more or less symbolic works self-consciously representing the "advanced" ideas of Greenwich Village: don't be staid, prudent, or traditional; be true to self. Women should be independent. Life should be a thing *really felt.* "The sensitive Dell," wrote Hutchins Hapgood, "expressed the spirit of the self-conscious woman of the time, the woman who accepts herself without the conventional lies thrust upon her by man's ancient imagination."[11]

Susan Glaspell's plays also set forth the claim of women to be regarded as men's equals. Feminism, broadly construed, had found many adherents from Sara Teasdale to Inez Milholland to Susan Glaspell to the militant suffrage workers who had been picketing the White House since January 10, 1917. Millay, graduated from Vassar during its era of reform, had come to the place where feminism was most highly regarded; and she herself, according to Floyd Dell, "was very much a revolutionary in all her sympathies, and a whole-hearted Feminist."[12]

The woman question was only one of a half dozen topics listed by Malcolm Cowley on which the Bohemians had reversed traditional opinions. (1) Only through self-expression can anyone attain to his full individuality. (2) Thus one must live intensely in the moment, regardless of decorum. (3) No obstacle to self-expression—no hindering convention or law—can be tolerated. (4) The body is not unclean; a pagan freedom of enjoyment in love should supplant former repressions. (5) One must reject social repressions that prevent children from realizing their potentialities, so that a pure, unthwarted generation can bring salvation to an outworn social order. (6) Obviously women must have freedom equal to men's. Cowley adds also the ideas of (7) psychological readjustment, chiefly through Freudian means, and (8) escaping Puritan bondage by going to Europe or other places unspoiled by Main Street taboos.[13] These ideas except those of salvation through the child and of psychological adjustment were part of Millay's credo.

Millay lived uncomfortably through the winter of 1917-18, working at her poems when she could find time and acting with the Provincetown Players. *Sweet and Twenty* opened January 25, 1918. During this period Floyd Dell was falling in love with the poet.[14] As their intimacy increased in the theater and during discussions of poetry and all the topics of the time, they were soon in the midst of an affair—a difficult, indecisive attachment, passionate, disturbing, and too filled with psychological reefs for them to reach calm harbor. Arthur Davison Ficke's account of

Millay's interpretation of her affair with Dell appears in his sonnet "Questioning a Lady":

> "His infinite curiosity too much pried
> Into that darkness which was mine alone.
> Sometimes I wished that I had merely died
> Before I let him think I was 'his own.'
> I am nobody's own. . . ."[15]

By Valentine's Day, Greenwich Village streets were practically rid of snow; but the poet's unmitigated poverty continued. On March 1, 1918, she wrote Harriet Monroe a note which she signed "Wistfully yours": "Spring is here,—and I could be very happy, except that I am broke. Would you mind paying me *now* instead of on publication for those so stunning verses of mine . . .? P. S. I am *awfully* broke. Would you mind paying me a lot?" The poems in question were a group of five light pieces entitled "Figs from Thistles," and Miss Monroe published them in the June issue of *Poetry*.

II *"I Was a Child, and You a Hero Grown"*

In February, 1918, Arthur Davison Ficke, then a major in the United States Army, and Millay's admirer, mentor, and friend through correspondence, passed through New York carrying military dispatches to France. Dell, who had known him in Davenport, Iowa, brought him to Waverly Place where Ficke met the author of "Renascence" for the first time. He and Dell, the Millay sisters, and Charles Ellis, Norma's beau, had a gay little party, sitting on the floor and eating sandwiches and pickles. Using as a first line a comment Norma made, "This pickle is a little loving cup," Ficke began improvising a sonnet.[16] His talent charmed the company but most significant was the impact that Vincent and Ficke had upon each other. Though the encounter was brief, though Ficke was married, and though he had to sail for France very soon,[17] emotional lightning had struck; and Millay was to "wear the red heart crumpled in the side" for the rest of her days. Both poets began writing sonnets inspired by their love.

The flaming of their passion, the quick consummation of love, and their being wrenched apart so violently constituted a devastating experience. Millay later admitted to Ficke: "My time, in those awful days after you went away to France, was a mist of thinking about you & writing sonnets to you.—You were spending your time in the same way, I believe.—That day before you sailed,—I shall never forget it. You were the first man I ever kissed without thinking that I should be sorry about it afterwards." She told him, too, that a sonnet he had asked about "was written both about you & about myself—we were both like that—but are not any more. The 'golden vessel of great song', also was written to you."

The sonnet written about both of them is number fourteen among Ficke's copies of Millay's sonnets in the Arthur Davison Ficke Collection in the Yale University Library:[18]

> I only know that every hour with you
> Is torture to me, and that I would be
> From your too poignant lovelinesses free!
> Rainbows, green flame, sharp diamonds, the fierce blue[19]
> Of shimmering ice-bergs, and to be shot through
> With lightning or a sword incessantly—
> Such things have beauty, doubtless; but to me
> Mist, shadow, silence—these are lovely too.
> There is no shelter in you anywhere;
> Rhythmic, intolerable, your burning rays
> Trample upon me, withering my breath;
> I will be gone, and rid of you, I swear:
> To stand upon the peaks of Love always
> Proves but that part of Love whose name is Death.

The sonnet, with its Pre-Raphaelite tone, expresses the protest against the pangs of passion and the binding power of her lover's "poignant lovelinesses" which was characteristic of Millay's independence: a desperate cry—"I will be gone"—wrung from her fear of utter domination.

"Into the golden vessel of great song" represents an attempt to sublimate this passion which is regarded as a common thing that, consummated, will leave the poet inarticulate. If "longing alone is singer to the lute," then the poets should continue to suffer and to long for the love "far and high" at the top of the tree. If one can pick up that fruit, with ease, from the ground, it will become a mere unvalued windfall. Millay's idealism speaks here—that high romantic estimate given to a pattern of perfection not embodied in the flesh. Yet her lover is her sun; whatever idealism and absence may do for the poet, for the woman it is bitter to resign herself to his loss. Her passion is strong, terrible, and permanent; and she is proud that this is so—an idea expressed in the emphatic sestet to "Let you not say of me when I am old":

> In me no lenten wicks watch out the night;
> I am the booth where Folly holds her fair;
> Impious no less in ruin than in strength,
> When I lie crumbled to the earth at length,
> Let you not say, "Upon this reverend site
> The righteous groaned and beat their breasts in prayer."

She felt that this love, too, would not last, any more than earlier loves had lasted; and perhaps she took solace from foreseeing a day when it would be gone, and he would recall ". . . that on the day you came/I was a child, and you a hero grown." Ultimately death would take him down: "And you as well must die, beloved dust, . . ./Nor shall my love avail you in your hour. . . ." She asserted finally that she was still resolved to dedicate her soul to poetry: she would not renounce it "for all the puny fever and frail sweat/Of human love." The body might have its nights of passion, but at the cost of betraying the lyre, keeping it silent; and for him to possess her soul was out of the question, for it would always return to its true home, Pieria, the "Singing Mountain" of the Muses (*CP*, 573-83). Thus, with a shelter of idealism combined with resignation, Vincent undertook to protect herself from the storm of her love for Arthur Ficke, which, it seems, assailed her more tempestuously than any other loves. Yet it would not die.

Though Ficke did not have the same problem of love versus career, he felt similarly the impact of pain and idealism, mixed hopelessness, agony, and exaltation:

> How savage is this destiny of ours
> That fashions music out of agony,
> And lets us hear, across the iron night,
> The wing-beats of each other's lonely flight.[20]

His counterpart to Millay's sonnets is his sonnet sequence "Beauty in Exile," in which their love is represented as beautiful, pathetically hopeless, and yet sublimely uplifting, so far is it above earthly things. They both regarded their devotion as permanent, unquestionable, and untouched by other concerns.

In September Vincent found another outlet for her work. Walter Adolphe Roberts had become editor of *Ainslee's* in 1918; and, since the publishers did not care what was used as fillers in the magazine, he resolved to "make the poetry in *Ainslee's* among the best printed in the United States."[21] Salomón de la Selva had told Roberts that Millay was an important poet who would become famous, so he invited her to contribute. She wrote him on September 12, 1918, that she would call the next week; when she came, she impressed him with her vividness and charm; she made him think of a tiger lily.

Roberts published many of her poems; but, since he could pay only fifty cents a line, she began to write short stories, and they "agreed that she should use the pseudonym Nancy Boyd for fiction. . . ." Her work appeared in nineteen consecutive issues of *Ainslee's*. For a year or more Roberts was among the men in love with her. He was jealous of the interest she showed in Pieter Mijer, a very handsome Dutch artist from the East Indies who introduced batik to America.[22]

In late summer, 1918, according to Floyd Dell, his affair with Millay was renewed; and she agreed to marry him.[23] The hearing for the second *Masses* trial was held on September 23, 1918; and the trial itself began on October 1. Dell, Eastman, the famous cartoonist Art Young, John Reed, and others were charged with "conspiring to promote insubordination and mutiny in the . . . forces of the United States and to obstruct recruiting and enlistment. . . ."[24] The penalty could have been as severe as twenty years in prison and a fine of $10,000. Dell had written: "There are some laws that the individual feels he cannot obey"; and he had upheld the "fundamental stubbornness of the free soul, against which all the powers of the State are helpless. . . ." Millay hated war; and to her the freedom of the soul constituted perhaps the highest of all values. She shared many of Dell's ideas, and she attended the trial with him. When for a second time the jury disagreed, the government had to give up its case.

Millay sympathized with socialist ideals. She told Grace King in 1941 that at the close of World War I "she had been in sympathy with the communist ideal of 'a free and equal society' but had never embraced the Communist Party. She had been 'almost a fellow-traveller with the communist idea as far as it went along with the socialist idea.' "[25] She was among those radicals who vehemently asserted the right, even the duty, of the individual to resist legislation that would in any way prevent the exercise of his rights of free expression, and to struggle to attain equality of opportunity for all. Dell wrote that he once gave Millay one of the bronze buttons awarded to women who were arrested for militant suffrage activities. With tears in her eyes she said, "I would rather have the right to wear this than anything I can think of."[26]

According to Dell, Millay was attracted to romantic, adventurous John Reed. Meanwhile, whether on account of Reed or not, her relations with Dell were difficult. She could never reconcile herself, it seemed, to the risk of subsiding, with marriage, into domesticity and being forced to give up her career—whether for lack of time or strength or on account of waning interest and inspiration. Although she had stirred him with lifelong effect, Dell lost hope of happiness with her, and their affair was broken off.[27]

Scudder Middleton, according to Allen Churchill, supplanted Dell as Millay's favorite.[28] Middleton, a poet with the romantic profile of a matinee idol, wrote anti-war, socialist poetry. For Middleton, Vincent wrote the classically inspired "To S. M. (If He Should Lie A-Dying)."

A main focus of her life that season was the Playwrights' Theatre. She directed *The Princess Marries the Page* on the first bill and took the leading role in it, played in George Cram Cook's hilarious *Tickless Time*, and had a Japanese role in *The String of the Samisen*, which opened January 17, 1919. There is, however, some question about whether she would have succeeded on the stage and how serious her attempts were to gain a place there. In 1931 she told Elizabeth Breuer: "I was awfully keen about acting. I might have done rather well with it if I had had proper direction. But I didn't have enough knowledge to sustain my effects."[29]

At the Provincetown she did have a chance to produce poetic drama and to direct and act in her own plays, but this work brought no income. Another theatrical possibility appeared when Lawrence Langner and some other Washington Square Players began discussing the idea of starting a new theater. Millay did not attend their first meeting (December 18, 1918) but joined in later discussions and became a member of the new Theatre Guild,[30] which decided to produce Jacinto Benavente's *The Bonds of Interest*. This *commedia dell'arte* costume play, laid in seventeenth-century Spain, was scheduled for April, and the part of Columbine was given to Millay. As Walter Prichard Eaton put it, she had a salary of "$25 a week, and a promise of sharing in the mythical profits. . . ."[31] The play met with qualified success. Wishing the new company well, critics gave it a fairly good reception; but the play hung on only four weeks. The future was not promising. Another opportunity came from the Washington Square Players: the leading role in Theresa Helburn's one-acter *Enter the Hero*—but evidently, as both Langner and Helburn indicate,[32] Millay's performance was not satisfactory. The play was withdrawn. Very likely because of this failure she was not given a part in the Theatre Guild's successful second production, *John Ferguson*.

Her income in this period came mainly from the "Nancy Boyd" stories in *Ainslee's*; but her chief satisfaction lay in poetry. During the early summer she worked on "Ode to Silence." In the fall she and Norma acted again in the Provincetown productions, and in November Vincent announced triumphantly to her mother that she had finished *Aria da Capo*—"You know the one, Pierrot & Columbine & the shepherds & the spirit of Tragedy.—Well, it's a peach. . . . Norma is going to play Columbine, & Charlie one of the shepherds." Millay directed *Aria da Capo*, which she had conceived three years earlier;[33] and it was the most distinguished offering of the Provincetown's 1919-20 season. Alexander Woollcott increased its success by his commendation in the *Times*,[34] and it presently took its place as an important contribution to American poetic drama.

III   *"I Am Most Faithless When I Most Am True"*

Soon after 1920 began, Millay wrote to a friend: "I am so tired these days—working terribly, terribly hard. . . ." Also her personal relations were complicated after she had met Edmund Wilson. He was already interested in her work and quickly fell in love with her and joined the array of her suitors, as did his friend and associate on the staff of *Vanity Fair*, John Peale Bishop.[35]

Millay traveled to Cincinnati during February to lecture and read from her work and gave other readings in New York. To Miss Rittenhouse she reported these activities and also the fact that she had three books ready to publish. But her greatest news was the welcome popularity of *Aria da Capo*, which had already been put on by several little theaters and published in *Reedy's Mirror*: "I find myself suddenly famous, Jessie, dear, and in this unlooked-for excitement I find a stimulant that almost takes the place of booze! . . . There is scarcely a little theatre or literary club in the country, so far as I can see, that isn't going to produce it or give a reading of it." Her correspondence, she said, had "been about doubled."[36] Small wonder that, with her writing, directing, correspondence, readings, preparing books for publication, and the amorous shocks of her personal life, she was "having a sort of nervous break-down," as she announced on April 7 to Allan Ross Macdougall.

The resurgence of fame must have given her undiluted pleasure, and to have sold a "Nancy Boyd" story to *Ainslee's* for four hundred dollars must have brought her not only a material satisfaction but a comfortable feeling of versatility. Kennerley was not bringing out her new volume (tentatively called *A Stalk of Fennel*) until fall. She was saddened to think of Bynner and Ficke far distant on a voyage to the Orient. To Ficke she confessed that she was "sodden with melancholy." And then: "There are so few people to whom one has a word to say, Arthur!" Though Edmund Wilson and others were ardently courting her, she was now too blasé to take much interest in them.

The four Millays moved to a house at Truro on Cape Cod for a summer of plain living, sea-winds, and sun. Wilson's courtship had reached a kind of *impasse*, if one may judge from Millay's letter of August 3, 1920; but she was interested enough to invite him for a week-end. However Wilson may have felt, he made the trip and formally proposed to her as they sat, tormented by Cape Cod mosquitoes, in a swing on the porch. She told him she would think it over. Next morning they talked with George Cram Cook and Hutchins Hapgood, and then went for a walk. Millay stared with her usual intensity at a lone egg that a gull had laid on the sand. Wilson later commemorated the experience in his "Provincetown":

> We never from the barren down,
>   Beneath the silver-lucid breast
> Of drifting plume, gazed out to drown
>   Where daylight whitens to the west.
>
> Here never in this place I knew
>   Such beauty by your side, such peace—
> These skies that, brightening, imbue
>   With dawn's delight the day's release.
>
> Only, upon the barren beach,
>   Beside the gray egg of a gull,
> With that fixed look and fervent speech,
>   You stopped and called it beautiful.
>
> Lone as the voice that sped the word!—
>   Gray-green as eyes that ate its round.—
> The desert dropping of a bird,
>   Bare-bedded in the sandy ground.
>
> Tonight, where clouds like foam are blown,
>   I ride alone the surf of light,
> As—even by my side—alone
>   That stony beauty burned your sight.[37]

The determined, desert loneliness of her life impressed Wilson; never for long, apparently, would she venture within the bounds of conventional expectation but had to follow her chosen rocky track—and not without pain. The intensity with which she lived every experience devoured her energies and left her prey to illness. Her thirtieth birthday not far ahead, she did not wish to eliminate the possibility of marriage; yet she did not wish to marry any of her suitors. As for some extra-marital arrangement of the Village type, she was not sanguine that the freedom it proffered in theory would hold up in practice without jealousy and unhappiness.[38]

Back in New York she was elated that *Vanity Fair* was featuring her work and that she received a prize of $100 from *Poetry* for "The Bean-Stalk." However, she was exasperated with Kennerley, who did not publish her books and who would neither answer letters nor talk to her on the telephone.[39] She would have liked to bring a suit against him.

On October 29, 1920, she wrote Ficke a deeply serious letter in an exalted tone, assuring him of her steadfast love. "I love you, too, my dear, and shall always, just as I did the first moment I saw you. You are a part of Loveliness to me. . . . It doesn't matter at all that we never see each other, & that we write so seldom. We shall never escape from each other." On the same day she asserted in a letter to Bynner that "the people of this country are just electing a new Sacred Goat." Though the women of the United States were able, because of the Nineteenth Amendment, to vote in national elections for the first time in 1920, Millay, however much a Feminist, was not impressed by the Harding-Cox encounter. In this attitude she was characteristic of her generation in the 1920's. They no longer believed in the ostensible aims of the war; they had no faith in public leaders; most intellectuals subsided into indifference to public affairs.[40]

The Jazz Age was beginning, the age in which the typical writer would say he detested politics, believed only in liberty, and could best be described as an anarchist; for "on principle he would fight to the death against Prohibition, censorship, blue laws and all that sort of thing."[41] Scott Fitzgerald spoke for the post-war generation: all through his work run the motifs of individualism and rebellion, transiency, excitement, and courage to follow absolutely one's own course. Presently Millay was to be regarded as the representative of that same generation.

Meanwhile, in the fall of 1920 she was being pulled down by illness—bronchitis—and then by "another small nervous breakdown." She was glad to take the opportunity to leave New York when it was presented to her.[42] Frank Crowninshield, editor of *Vanity Fair*, proposed that she go to Europe, free to write what she pleased, under either her own name or her *nom de plume*, Nancy Boyd. She was to have a regular salary.[43] She explained to Mrs. Millay: ". . . My work, more than anything else, my poetry, I mean, needs fresh grass to feed on. I am becoming sterile here; I have known it would be, & I see it approaching if I stay here.— Also, New York life is getting too congested for me,—too many people; I get no time to work."

IV "I Wanted Every Bit of the Experience"

Before sailing January 4, 1921, on the *Rochambeau*, Millay practiced French.[44] She was proud of speaking French and especially proud of not becoming seasick. Though she had bought some remedies for seasickness, she had refused to take them. She wrote her mother, most significantly: "I wanted every bit of the experience, & no dope. (Like you, when I was going to be born.)" This avidity for sharply felt experience, the welcoming of the fullness of life at whatever cost, evidently passed from mother to daughter; and, regarded as a badge of honor, it was a deep, important part of Millay's personality.

Her itinerary from July 21, 1921, to February, 1923, included stays in Paris; Hertfordshire, England; Albania; Italy; Vienna; Budapest. Like most travelers, Millay at first felt keenly the emotion created by places with romantic traditions and the excitement of seeing new things. Later, her emotions became tempered by familiarity and illness, and she experienced loneliness perhaps oftener than she would willingly admit; she frequently asked for more letters from home.

Even in Europe she still had her living to earn. In March, 1921, she was "slaving" to type her play *The Lamp and the Bell* for the Vassar alumnae; in May she was "working like the devil"; in July she was planning to write a *Vanity Fair* article on the difference between American and English idioms; in September she was hoping to finish her "long sonnet sequence about the New England woman," and was looking forward to her next book, which she said was "going to be dam [sic] good." She had recently completed "The Ballad of the Harp-Weaver," but she wrote little poetry; poetically, the year in Europe was to be a fallow one. In November, 1922, she was congratulating herself because the Nancy Boyd articles had practically supported her for nearly two years.

Other American writers were visiting Europe while she was there. At jazz parties and in the cafes of Montparnasse, where there was almost an American colony, Millay saw these people as they passed through; but it does not seem that she made contact Europeans or that her European sojourn provided her with the kind of intellectual excitement that some of her younger compatriots experienced. To friends in the Village there later came rumors of love affairs she had in Europe. The most serious of them, apparently, was with a young Frenchman.[45]

Regardless of love affairs and even though she was one of the "hard-working, Paris-mad,/Eager, blasé, young imbeciles!" (*CP*, 414), she often sent her thoughts homeward and reckoned the time she had been away. "I am awfully faithful to my immediate family," she wrote after nine months. In a letter of June 15, 1921, she rejoiced in her mother's success at writing and in the youthful spirit that led her to have her "old cute head bobbed." The letter is explicit about her feeling for Mrs. Millay and about her indebtedness to her mother. Millay's deep love and her consciousness that her mother had, through hard work and self-sacrifice, imposed limitations upon herself; and her appreciation for all that her mother had provided for her inspired Millay to suggest on July 23 that she come to Europe the next fall or winter, if Millay could earn enough money. She brought up the idea again on September 5, but she then thought the trip would have to wait until spring. Meanwhile, other happenings intervened to make her mother's coming seem improbable. During Vincent's nearly four-week sally into far-off Albania, her lonely heart was overcome once more by love for Arthur Ficke. All she could think of to write him was: "Why aren't you here? Oh, why aren't you here? . . . I tell you I must see you again.—"

The years were flying by. In New York she had told Edmund Wilson, "I'll be thirty in a minute!"[46] Upon returning from Albania to Rome, she learned of Norma's marriage to Charles Ellis, which made her happy but also made her think: "Well, both my little sisters are young married women, and me, I am just about three months from being an old maid. . . ."

After a short time in Rome, chilled by the autumnal damp and looking "paler and more delicate than ever,"[47] she went to Vienna where she lived in a cheap, dismal room. As she wrote Ficke on December 10, she was in one of her "periodic states of being entirely busted." On the same day she sent some poems to the *Yale Review*, saying rather wistfully: "I hope you will like something here.—I wish you could print the Liberty Bell but suppose you couldn't." On December 31 she had an acceptance of two of the poems and a check for $3 (a mistake for $30). More than a month passed before the error was rectified.[48] Millay was dispirited.

Just before Christmas the possibility of marriage had suddenly arisen. The proposal came, but not directly, from Witter Bynner. An all-important letter from him was lost, and the only inkling Millay had of the proposal was the implication of a note from Ficke with a postscript by Bynner. In a pleasant and, naturally, rather cautious letter of December 23, she agreed to marry him. The idea was not new to her; she had thought during the summer of 1920 that she might marry him some day. Through the next two months they considered the possibility of marriage but eventually gave it up.

On March 1, 1922, things happened that caused Millay's perspective to change. She had projected a novel to be called *Hardigut*; in fact, while in Rome, she had had several conferences about it with Sinclair Lewis, who was scouting manuscripts for Alfred Harcourt.[49] She received on the morning of March 1 a five-hundred-dollar advance on the novel from Horace Liveright. Norma informed her that Mrs. Millay had been ill and felt disappointed over the postponement of her projected trip. Millay at once decided it was essential to bring her mother to Europe, and she put $400 into Mrs. Millay's hands.

In Paris that spring Millay took her mother "everywhere, on all my rough parties," both of them "doing the whole darn town, like a couple of flat-footed tourists. . . ." They spent the summer and the fall in England, living in a small thatched house in a Dorsetshire village, taking long walks and making expeditions to various cities. Millay gradually regained better spirits.

Ficke's marriage had broken up, as he had earlier let her know. She was able to admire the riding and painting of his fiancée, Gladys Brown, who happened to be staying in the same village. Millay proudly reasserted her love for Ficke; but she told him she had been thinking "of Mrs. Fate and Mr. Gord, & other star parts in this Hicktown meller-drammer full of worn-out jokes entitled, 'Life, or Ain't it Hell to be Thirsty.'"

She was supposed to be working on *Hardigut* for spring publication. In fact, Liveright put out a dummy of the proposed novel with a dust-jacket carrying a letter she wrote him in November. She told him that she was finishing it in Dorset and that it would be ready for publication in April. The characters of her book—evidently a sort of philosophical novel to be classified with Butler's *Erewhon* or certain works of Anatole France—were to live in a country where no one could "eat in public, or discuss food except in inuendos [sic] and with ribald laughter; where for unmarried people to eat anything at all is scandalous; where young boys and girls struggle through a starved adolescence into a hasty and ill-assorted marriage; where the stomach is never mentioned. . . ."[50] *Hardigut* might have had overtones of Cabell; for *love* one reads *eat*; for *sex, food.* She told Liveright it would be "amusing, satiric, ugly, beautiful, poetic, and an unmistakable allegory." According to Grace Hegger Lewis, Millay thought it would surely be suppressed.[51] Millay intended to finish it—probably one should say, write it; for she told Norma on November 10, 1922, that, although she had made Liveright think it was nearly done, she would have to write it in the south of France. Also she was glad that Floyd Dell liked "The Poet and His Book"—"I'm so tired of hearing about Renascence I'm nearly dead."

She and her mother went to the south of France in December; apparently she felt briefly revitalized at Cassis-sur-Mer, but she told Ficke on December 17 that what strength she had must go into the novel. She had envisioned a homecoming in June after trips to Italy and again to England, but she and her mother returned in February, 1923.[52] Shortly thereafter she said in an interview that the young people everywhere were "going to change things" and that America, though artistically awake, was "rubbing its eyes and saying 'Where am I?' I believe . . . if it finds itself in a prison it will not say 'I am in a lovely garden.' I hope these young people will not be afraid of the truth."[53] Her radicalism remained unchanged.

CHAPTER 3

'A Growing Heart to Feed'

B Y 1923 Millay's chief publications were *Renascence and Other Poems, Aria da Capo, A Few Figs from Thistles*, and *Second April*. She had also published various stories, sketches, and dialogues, some under her own name, some under "Nancy Boyd." Frank Shay had persuaded her to let him issue *A Few Figs*. After much delay Kennerley finally published a volume of more serious poems with the title of *Second April* in 1921. In spite of her illnesses, Millay was able to publish several poems during 1922. The *Yale Review* did not take "To the Liberty Bell"; so she sent it to Floyd Dell for the *Liberator*, where it appeared in October. Working with Frank Shay and Millay's sister Kathleen, Dell also selected four poems to add to *A Few Figs* for an enlarged edition; but he could not find many in the manuscripts that were light enough in tone.[1] During 1922 Millay became a member of a group of poets who sponsored *American Poetry: A Miscellany*, a cooperative venture started in 1920 as a biennial volume. Millay used her space in the *Miscellany* for eight sonnets.[2] She also issued her *Ballad of the Harp-Weaver* as a pamphlet. On the basis of these poems published in 1922 she was awarded the Pulitzer Prize for Poetry in 1923.

I ". . . *Such a Man as Any Wife Would Pass a Pretty Lad for*"

In New York, Millay found herself exhausted and still afflicted by illness. In the spring of 1923 she made a weekend visit to Croton-on-Hudson with her friend Esther Root. At Croton—then "a kind of literary and political shrine," a sort of "suburb of Washington Square"[3]—a group of liberals and radicals had made homes along Mount Airy Road for themselves: John Reed, Max Eastman, Eugen Boissevain, Boardman Robinson, Floyd Dell, Stuart Chase, and Dudley Field Malone. Millay attended a party given by Malone, defender of the suffragists, and Doris Stevens, militant suffragist author. When the company played charades, Millay and Eugen Boissevain were paired to act the parts of lovers. They acted with extraordinary conviction; in fact, Dell and the rest of the company watched Millay and Boissevain actually falling in love.[4]

Handsome, powerful, and boisterous, a forty-three-year-old widower once married to Inez Milholland, Boissevain was the son of a Dutch newspaper owner and an Irish mother. As a youth he had visited the United States and been received at the White House by Theodore Roosevelt. An athlete, he had rowed in the Henley Regatta. He was given to frank expression: after being psychoanalyzed by Jung in Zurich, he developed "the art of casually blurting out . . . the intimate truth." He entered business in the United States, handling details of Marconi's enterprises and later becoming an importer of sugar, cotton, and coffee; but he was imaginative, enjoyed being with creative people, and was a dedicated advocate of feminism.[5] Loving and pitying the poet, this big protective man took Millay, very ill the day after the party, into his house to nurse her; and he assumed responsibility for seeing that she had the systematic medical attention she needed. Dell thought that his devoted care perhaps saved her life.[6]

Meanwhile her dissatisfaction with Kennerley led her to make a permanent connection with Harper and Brothers. She signed a contract for the publication of her new collection of poems, and Ficke helped her in April, 1923, with the problem of rights to earlier books. He drew up a tentative contract according to which Harper was to acquire the title to *Renascence* and *Second April* from Kennerley by purchase, or "commence an action or proceeding" against him to acquire "all the rights of said Kennerley, if any, in and to the said books and for an accounting for past royalties due the author." This contract never became effective;[7] but it indicates the line taken by Millay to escape from the unprofitable connection with Kennerley.

Her fatigue and illness continued. But on May 30 she announced to her mother that she loved Eugen Boissevain and was going to marry him. "There!!!" Boissevain took her to doctors; and they advised an operation, which was appointed for July 18. That morning Boissevain decided that she must enter the hospital as his wife; accordingly, a justice of the peace was summoned, they were married, and in the afternoon they drove to a New York hospital.

During that summer of illness and convalescence from the operation, Millay made an adaptation of Molnár's play *Heavenly and Earthly Love* (under the title of *Launzi*). Ficke "did a great deal of work" helping her ready *The Harp-Weaver and Other Poems* for the press. On August 30, 1923, she dictated to him her sonnet "I see so clearly now my similar years": "She had never put a word of it on paper before, but had composed it entirely in her head, as she often does."[8]

II ". . . *A Dream That Wanders Wide and Late*"

In November, Millay "went down to Washington to see the President—with a whole bunch of suffragists—also to read a poem which [she] had written, at a conference thingumajig in the Capitol." This was the final ceremony arranged by the National Women's Party to commemorate the seventy-fifth anniversary of the Equal Rights meeting of 1848 in Seneca Falls. At noon, November 17, 1923, a deputation from the Party called on the President. On the next day at a ceremony in the Crypt of the Capitol, a statue was unveiled in honor of Lucretia Mott, Susan B. Anthony, and Elizabeth Cady Stanton. Introduced by her friend Doris Stevens, Millay, "foremost woman poet of America, stirred the audience with a poem she had written for the occasion, and was called back to read it a second time," *Equal Rights* reported, printing both her sonnet "The Pioneer" and her picture.[9] In her *Collected Sonnets* Millay entitled the sonnet "To Inez Milholland" —a gracious tribute by Eugen Boissevain's second wife to his first: "I, that was proud and valiant, am no more;—/Save as a dream that wanders wide and late. . . ." But more significant in 1923 was the call to further action: "Only my standard on a taken hill/Can cheat the mildew. . . ." Millay's Feminism persisted: she was honored among those who continued the agitation for equal rights; and her name appeared as an Associate Editor of *Equal Rights* in the issue of April 19, 1924, with Zona Gale, Phyllis Duganne, Inez Hayes Irwin, and Crystal Eastman.

The reading tour of January-February, 1924, she found difficult because of the discomforts of trains, the grossness of other travelers, and the inefficiency of hotels—difficulties she reported in a wryly humorous way to her husband. She took pleasure in certain "sweet & real people"; but at times before philistine audiences she "felt like a prostitute"; and by February 5, 1924, though she was successful with her readings, she had become tired, dull, and "sunk in a lethargy of boredom. . . ." One feels in her letters the artist's irritation with the middle class and especially with the Middle West: "the puritanic moral code and the empty commercial drive, which . . . dominated these people."[10] But she endured this work to earn money to pay debts and to help her mother. In succeeding years her husband generally accompanied her; in 1924 she was buoyed up by the prospect of a trip to the Orient in the spring.

III   *"And Who Are These That Dive for Copper Coins?"*

The Boissevains left San Francisco on a Japanese ship about April 19, 1924.[11] Their tour took them round the world: Honolulu, Japan, China, Hong Kong, Java, Singapore, India, Marseilles, and Paris. Her letters during the tour are usually exuberant with appreciation of tropical beauty, foreign scenery and customs, and returning health. On May 6 in Tokyo she wrote an amusing little preface for *Distressing Dialogues* (by Nancy Boyd) in which she said: "I take pleasure in recommending to the public these excellent small satires, from the pen of one in whose work I have a never-failing interest and delight."

Only a few of her poems appear to have a connection with her world tour: "For Pao-Chin, a Boatman on the Yellow Sea," which appeared in *The Buck in the Snow*; "To a Calvinist in Bali" in *Huntsman, What Quarry?*; Sonnet 31 of *Fatal Interview* with the line "And who are these that dive for copper coins" (she remarked how at Honolulu "the water about the ship was black with the heads of native boys swimming about & diving for coins which the passengers threw into the water"); and Sonnets 7 and 8 of "Epitaph for the Race of Man."

IV *"Between the Red-Top and the Rye"*

The year 1925 brought two significant experiences: moving from New York to a farm, and working on a libretto for an opera. Boissevain cared little for his importing business and was agreeable to buying a seven-hundred-acre, run-down farm in the Berkshire foothills at Austerlitz, New York. They named the place "Steepletop" for the showy pink flower abounding in their meadows. Steepletop became their base of operations for the rest of their lives.

On May 5 and 6 Millay participated in an Institute of Modern Literature at Bowdoin College as part of the celebration of the Bowdoin Centennial. She read from her poems in a packed hall, acted all parts of *Two Slatterns and a King*, and won an ovation.[12] On June 15 she received her first honorary degree: a Litt.D. from Tufts College.

Having been commissioned by the Metropolitan to compose an opera, Deems Taylor approached the poet for a libretto that she promptly agreed to write. For most of 1925 she tried to make a libretto on the story of Snow White and the Seven Dwarfs.[13] While she and Boissevain were occupied with the problems of Steepletop, her letters display energy and high spirits although from July 28 on she reported that she had a constant headache and spots before her eyes. She gaily announced that she would take Carter's Little Liver Pills for a while longer before going "over to Swamproot or Lydia Pinkham's well-known stirrup-cup." She began to complain of people who wrote to her desiring readings, advice about writing, autographs, special permission to reprint poems, and the like. Fame and publicity were apparently bringing their disadvantages.

Toward Christmas she scrapped the one act she had written on the Snow White libretto and began work on a story of tenth-century England from the *Gesta Regum Anglorum* of William of Malmesbury. She tentatively called it *The Saxons* but finally entitled it *The King's Henchman*. Over the signature of Nancy Boyd, she also found time to send to Franklin P. Adams's *Conning Tower* a poem called "The Armistice Day Parade," for which Adams awarded a watch for the best contribution of the year. The poem, reprinted in the *Literary Digest* (December 19, 1925), illustrates the anti-war sentiments of many liberals of the 1920's:

> "I shall not march," said the Major,
> In the Armistice Day parade."
>
> .   .   .   .
>
> "Peace on Earth is a fine ideal
> But men are human and life is real.
>
> .   .   .   .
>
> "Take a man like me," said the Major,
>
> .   .   .   .
>
> "He must have a little war now and then—
> I mean, of course, a war of defense—
> Or he can't digest his meals.
> And now here come these pacifist Yids
> And drag in peace, and spoil the procession.
>
> Good Lord, a soldier's wife and kids
> Have got to eat, and war's a profession
> Same as [the] clergy," said the Major.
> "If you went and abolished war," said he,
> "Where in hell would the army be?"

The poem resulted from a concern over growing militarism. The next issue of the *Literary Digest* carried news of protests against militarism in the schools: "students are being taught that 'war is natural, war is human, war is inevitable.'"

Snowed in—"hermetically"—for several winter weeks at Steepletop, Millay continued work on her libretto, still afflicted by headaches and "dancing dark spots." She sent the libretto to Deems Taylor, scene by scene. He composed a piano score and completed the orchestration later in Paris.[14]

For nearly a year Arthur and Gladys Ficke had been living in Santa Fe (where Bynner had made his home for several years) because Ficke had developed tuberculosis. They invited the Boissevains for a visit and included the fare both ways. The Boissevains started October 23; in Santa Fe, Millay worked hard, with Ficke's help, on the final revision of the proofs of *The King's Henchman*, which she sent off December 6. Early in 1927, back at Steepletop, she wrote "To the Wife of a Sick Friend"; it appeared in *The Buck in the Snow*.[15]

The early weeks of 1927 were filled with growing excitement over the premiere of *The King's Henchman*, a memorable production occurring on February 17 with Edward Johnson, Lawrence Tibbett, and Tullio Serafin as conductor. The audience became increasingly enthusiastic over this brilliant American opera written in English with a poetic quality most unusual in a libretto. Composer and librettist received an ovation at the end of the performance. The applause was equally heavy at a second performance on February 21. A road company took the opera on tour for several months, and it was seen at the Metropolitan fourteen times during three seasons. As a play, *The King's Henchman* went through three printings in three weeks; by November, it was in its eighteenth printing. Millay had reached another crest of success and fame.[16]

V *"Justice Denied"*

On April 18, 1927, Millay sent to Elinor Wylie an expostulation to be forwarded to the League of American Penwomen. Because of their "recent gross and shocking insolence to one of the most distinguished writers of our time," she no longer felt honored by an invitation from the League. She continued stiffly:

> It is not in the power of an organization which has insulted Elinor Wylie, to honour me.
> And indeed I should find it unbecoming on my part, to sit as Guest of Honour in a gathering of writers, where honour is tendered not so much for the excellence of one's literary accomplishment as for the circumspection of one's personal life.
> Believe me, if the eminent object of your pusillanimous attack has not directed her movements in conformity with your timid philosophies, no more have I mine. I too am eligible for your disesteem. Strike me too from your lists, and permit me, I beg you, to share with Elinor Wylie a brilliant exile from your fusty province.

Millay's integrity, loyalty, sense of justice, and admiration of independence brought forth this crackling letter, so formal, stiff,
and devastatingly sarcastic.

In the summer of 1927 the Sacco-Vanzetti case was causing
more and more concern among liberals the world over. Nicola
Sacco and Bartolomeo Vanzetti, Italians and anarchists both, had
been arrested, tried, and convicted of murder and robbery of a
paymaster and his guard, a crime committed April 15, 1920, at
South Braintree, Massachusetts. It was widely felt that the Italians
were victims of post-war anti-radical hysteria and of the prejudice
of Judge Webster Thayer. For six years their lawyers had staved
off their execution. In the latter part of 1926 suggestions had been
made that Governor Alvin T. Fuller of Massachusetts appoint an
advisory committee to re-investigate the case.[17]

Governor Fuller was petitioned for a stay of execution and an
order for an investigation. With the petition were filed affidavits
alleging prejudice on the part of Judge Thayer.[18] Fuller started
an investigation of the case and on June 1 appointed an advisory
committee of three. The advisory committee submitted a report
to Governor Fuller on July 27, and the Governor announced on
August 3 that the report coincided with the result of his own investigation: Sacco and Vanzetti were guilty and must die.[19] The
following day there was a "world stir" over the decision. Defense
attorneys criticized the secrecy of the inquiry; protest meetings
were held; and in France, Henry Wadsworth Dana, "an American,
who recently has been prominent at French Communist gather-
ings," presented a motion for a twenty-four-hour general strike in
protest. Presently the American Civil Liberties Union protested.[20]

Judge Thayer refused to withdraw from the hearing (before
himself) on his own prejudice in the case. On August 9 he denied motions for a stay of execution. Appeals, protests, and world-
wide demonstrations could not save the condemned men; but
Governor Fuller gave them a reprieve until August 22.[21] On
August 20, all efforts having failed, Boston sympathizers sent out
a wire: "Picketers urgently needed to picket State House beginning Saturday morning until the execution of Sacco and Vanzetti.
It is all we can do now. Will you come and bring anyone you can
for that service."[22] To this appeal Millay responded. If she had

not been concerned over Sacco and Vanzetti in 1920-21, she had been concerned over the weakening of America's free-speech tradition, as "To the Liberty Bell" attests:

> They say we have no leader now. It may be.
> I know
> We have no cause.
>
> America!—Beautiful Nowhere in the hearts of a few
> Periwigged men
> Sitting about a table.
>
> Toll, toll.
>
> Yet toll not.
> Lest to our shame we learn how few to-day
> Would stand in the street and listen.
>
> Only some lean, half-hearted anarchist
>
> Who happened to be out;
> And the children,
> That shout at air-planes.[23]

As the hopes for the condemned men grew more desperate, Millay put into Ruth Hale's hands her poem "Justice Denied in Massachusetts," written "as her contribution to the registering of the feeling many of us have about the Sacco-Vanzetti execution." Miss Hale (Heywood Broun's wife) sent the poem to the *New York Times*, where it was printed August 22. Millay's feeling that under the black cloud of injustice the precious American inheritance was blighted, never to grow again, must have been felt by many. The poem is based on the same concept as "To the Liberty Bell": American ideals of liberty had been betrayed in the twentieth century.

On Sunday, August 21, the entire Boston police force was called out, and the militia as well. The traditional use of Boston Common for speeches was denied, though thousands gathered there; and picketers were arrested.[24] The execution was to be immediately after midnight of August 22, and on that day Millay and her husband were in Boston with thousands of others. Across the Common from the State House a continual protest meeting was being held at Scenic Temple: groups of a dozen or so people would leave to picket the State House, only to be arrested. While members of the American Legion uttered catcalls and hisses, picketers carrying placards and banners marched in single file to the State House; the police warned them that they were "sauntering and loitering" and after seven minutes hauled them in patrol wagons to the Joy Street Station. Near the head of a group of thirteen writers and poets Millay marched, with Powers Hapgood and John Dos Passos. She carried a placard with the inscription: "If these men are executed, justice is dead in Massachusetts." More than one hundred fifty picketers were arrested during the day, squeezed into a hot bail room, finally bailed out at $25 each. Boissevain gave bail for his wife, and they aided others with bail when money ran short.

That afternoon Millay had an audience with Governor Fuller, to whom she told a story she had heard about the last hanging in Maine. Two men accused of murder with strong evidence against them had in their favor only the testimony of a fisherman. They were convicted and executed, for the governor would not intercede. Later the murderer confessed. Governor Fuller said he would think about what she had told him.

That evening the crowd in Scenic Temple accepted Ruth Hale's proposal that they "gather during the evening in Salem Street, in the shadow of the Old North Church, . . . and listen to Miss Millay's reading of her poem 'Justice Is Dead.' " Presumably, Millay read the poem there. Later in the evening Millay and Boissevain were with other sympathizers in a room at the Bellevue Hotel. She withdrew to the next room and composed a final appeal to Governor Fuller. According to Arthur Garfield Hays, it was hurried to the State House at 11:40 and was delivered. In the latter part of her eloquent letter Millay wrote:

> You promised me, and I believed you truly, that you would think of what I said. I exact of you this promise now. Be for a moment alone with yourself. Look inward upon yourself. Let fall from your harassed mind, all, all save this: which way would He have turned, this Jesus of your faith?
>
> I cry to you with a million voices: answer our doubt. Exert the clemency which your high office affords.
>
> There is need in Massachusetts of a great man tonight. It is not yet too late for you to be that man.

But Governor Fuller remained silent, and Sacco and Vanzetti were executed a few minutes after midnight.[25]

All picketers arrested were found guilty on August 23 of violating Boston ordinances; all but six paid a fine of five dollars each. Millay and five others were fined ten dollars each, and they appealed. Arthur Garfield Hays said he would carry the cases to the Supreme Court, if necessary, for an interpretation of ordinances on sauntering and loitering in connection with peaceful persuasion. In October, Millay went again to Boston in connection with the case, but the trial was postponed. The defendants were acquitted December 3, 1927.[26]

Because of her health, Millay returned to Steepletop and did not participate in the "death march" three days after the execution, when Sacco and Vanzetti were buried. On August 24 Hays made public Millay's letter to Governor Fuller. The next day the New York *World* printed a letter from Edmund Pearson showing errors in the story Millay had told Fuller about the "last hanging" in Maine. She then set to work, getting more material on the matter from her mother, and prepared a reply to Pearson, which was published in the *World* on October 6. She demonstrated that Pearson had also made errors, as had other people discussing executions in Maine. She took these mistakes, her own included, as evidence "that human beings with the best intentions in the world often made mistakes," and concluded: "that Governor Fuller himself made a mistake is very far from impossible."[27]

Millay continued working hard during October, writing poetry and the article "Fear" which was published in *The Outlook*, November 9, 1927. It began:

> There are two names you would not have me mention, for you are sick of the sound of them. All men must die, you say, and these men have died, and would that their names might die with them. . . . *Do* let us forget, you say; after all, what *does* it matter?
>
> You are right; it does not matter very much. . . . In a freedom already so riddled and gashed by the crimes of the state this ugly rent is with difficulty to be distinguished at all.

After a strong poetic expression of the inevitability of death, Millay declared that there was tumult in the minds of the young, who saw through the hypocrisies of their elders. The war had disillusioned them and made them avid for pleasure. "As for their illusions, well, they have seen you at war, and they are beginning to understand why you went to war; they have seen you engaged in many another dubious and embarrassing activity; and now they have seen this." She attacked the "unkindness, hypocrisy, and greed" of the elders—"these are the forces that shall bring us low and enslave our children." Although she was not idealistic enough to be an anarchist, she could speak because she possessed "that simple right of the citizen to hold any opinions he may choose and to express any opinions he may hold"—though such expression contrary to majority opinion was dangerous, and had cost that nameless pair their lives. She could say these things because she no longer cared so much about her inviolate personal life. In her bitterness even death might be a comfort. The beauty of the physical world "can no longer at such moments make up to me at all for the ugliness of man, his cruelty, his greed, his lying face."

Millay's bitter opinions were the accepted views of radicals who thought that the United States had entered the war for materialistic reasons and who were affronted and alarmed by A. Mitchell Palmer's Red-hunt, the unfair union-smashing devices of big business, vigilante terrorizing by the Ku Klux Klan, and the general intensification of "100 per cent Americanism."[28] Such views appeared unpatriotic to many *Outlook* readers, some forty of whom immediately wrote, mostly in protest, to the editor, who had to defend (in the issue of November 23, 1927) the propriety of printing the article, against an attack by a man who said it was "fit only for a most rabid Socialistic magazine." Millay was comforted by a letter from Bynner, and could write proudly to her mother: "What made you think Eugen would be picking on me, or on you, about this matter? He has been perfectly magnificent through this whole thing, as you ought to know he would be."

Millay told Grace King in 1941 that the Sacco-Vanzetti case revealed to her the underground workings of those who "would sell self, honor and religion to keep in power." The affair deepened her disillusionment with mankind—already evinced in *Aria da Capo*—and increased her scorn for the American public. It also made her social consciousness more specific: she became "more aware of the underground workings of forces alien to true democracy."[29]

VI "A House on Upland Acres"

At Steepletop the poet had a refuge against vulgar encroachment upon her creative hours and against the shocks of worldly encounters. Though the farm was remote and had been run-down, its new owners gradually turned it into a modest chateau. Boissevain removed from his wife's shoulders all workaday responsibilities, exercising the functions of husband, lover, farm overseer, business manager, secretary, and at times a whole staff of servants. Their life in the hills could be as rurally dull as they desired; but actually, with farm improvement, some social life, the stimulation of reading, occasional trips to New York, and a considerable amount of more extensive travel, Millay's life had a good deal of variety.

Boissevain hired a French couple for farm work, for cooking and household duties, and especially for the laying down of a cellarful of wine. But it was difficult to keep servants in the country; when they left, he cooked and attended to other household details with no loss of equanimity.[30] A believer in Feminism and the husband of two such gifted women, he formulated a model philosophy for the mate of a woman of genius. Millay's poetic task was "to immortalize the beauty of the moment," and consequently "she must ever remain open to contact with life's intensities." He solved their problem simply by managing all the "quotidian matters" because "it is so obvious that Vincent is more important than I am. Anyone can buy and sell coffee. . . ." He also tried to make their marriage an adventure, with no feeling of assured possession but of love maintained with "a terrific and continuous excitement."[31]

Her privacy and freedom for writing assured, Millay could retire at will to her upstairs study, and there, under a sign reading SILENCE, she created poems in her ten-cent notebooks. For years the Boissevains were without a telephone; they seldom saw newspapers. Millay would come down at times to work in her flower gardens or to play the piano. She regretted leaving the ocean; so they spent some summer weeks in Maine each year; and after the summer of 1933, when they bought Ragged Island in Casco Bay, they had a salt-water hideaway.[32]

They maintained cordial relations with a good many friends, and Millay was glad to help other writers as her strength permitted. On December 27, 1927, she wrote a tactful letter to an old friend and Sunday-school teacher Abbie Huston Evans, making suggestions about the revision and publication of Miss Evans's poems. She recommended that Stephen Vincent Benét be given a Guggenheim Fellowship in 1926, and made the same recommendation later for E. E. Cummings and Kay Boyle. She wrote out a detailed criticism of Edmund Wilson's novel *I Thought of Daisy* in 1929.[33] When Llewelyn Powys was under heavy expense relating to his conviction for libel, Millay and Boissevain sent a cablegram from St. Thomas, February 6, 1935: "You will receive thousand within fortnight second thousand about week later more available if necessary. . . ."[34] A month later she reassured Powys about her ability to send so much money and chided him for being reluctant to accept it. Sensitive to the feelings of writers she respected, she tried to be considerate and wise in her dealings with them.

Over a period of eight or ten years she spent some twenty per cent of her time in travel. There were reading tours some years in the fall and early winter. The publication of her books continued; *Fatal Interview* was the greatest success after *The King's Henchman*. Although she was occasionally stricken by illnesses, mostly respiratory, Millay had the satisfaction of certain new honors and activities that are listed in the Chronology.

While her successes were accumulating, death, "the Canker in the Leaf," could strike. Millay was grief-stricken by the death of Elinor Wylie on December 16, 1928, and wrote a tender letter of sympathy to the bereaved husband, William Rose Benét. Further sadness came with the death of her mother on February 5, 1931; the burial of Mrs. Millay took place at Steepletop a week later.[35] Vincent commemorated both women in poems and dedicated *Fatal Interview* to Elinor Wylie.

During these years of comparative luxury, a translation of Baudelaire's *Flowers of Evil* was begun—a joint endeavor of Millay and George Dillon. They had met in late 1928 when he had introduced her for a reading at the University of Chicago, a brilliantly successful occasion. He had shown her some translations of Baudelaire he had made, and she urged him to publish a book of them. When he inquired jokingly whether she would write a preface for the book, she said she would be delighted. In the spring of 1935 she sent him two or three translations she had done and said she would like to have them included with his, if he published them. Then she became absorbed in translating; when Dillon visited Steepletop that summer, intensive work enabled her to finish drafts of numerous translations already begun and to write part of a preface. Dillon had been swept along by her enthusiasm for publication, and presently negotiations were concluded with Harper.

Dillon and the Boissevains then went to Maine for a week, after which the poet and her husband embarked for Europe in September, 1935. Millay made investigations in France regarding Baudelaire and consulted with her friend Lucie Delarue-Mardrus, a poet and novelist, about the translations and about French critical opinion on Baudelaire. She arrived again in New York on October 13 and busied herself at Steepletop and at Delray Beach, Florida, until past New Year's with proofreading, layout, the preface, and biographical notes to accompany the translation.[36] Then she concentrated on *Conversation at Midnight* and finished it by May, 1936.

VII *"The Whole Round World Rolling in Darkness"*

When, on May 2, 1936, Millay looked up from the beach of Sanibel Island, Florida, and saw the Palms Hotel in flames, she quickly realized that she had lost the manuscript of her new book, *Conversation at Midnight*. She and her husband struggled back to Steepletop by car, and she started to set the poems down again, as accurately as she could. Her troubles were increased because of an injury to her back that occurred during the summer of 1936 when the door of a station-wagon had opened and she had been pitched out and had rolled down a rocky gully. Her right arm was frequently useless; and, after the source of the pain was recognized, she was involved with doctors and operations until late in 1941.

Her peace of mind and her principles were subjected to great stress during these years. Her Feminist principles flashed out as usual in her 1937 protest to New York University authorities over not being included among the male recipients of honorary degrees at a dinner given by the chancellor. At this time she was working on a translation of a Spanish poem honoring García Lorca for an anthology entitled *And Spain Sings*; this effort was for the benefit of the Spanish Loyalists. She was disturbed by the Spanish Civil War, by the increasing Nazi-Fascist encroachments on liberty, and by the growing certainty of general war, its arrival, and, finally, American participation in it.

In 1941 Millay told Grace King: "Eight years ago I was an ardent pacifist, a true conscientious objector. My thought and opinion were that it was wrong to go to arms."[38] However, the failure of the League of Nations to prevent Japan's attack on China and Italy's conquest of Ethiopia, the Nazi dismemberment and succeeding occupation of Czechoslovakia, and the German-Russian non-aggression treaty of August 23, 1939, brought about a change in Millay's outlook and finally convinced her "that no course of action other than the sternest resistance" was possible.[39]

Millay spoke at the New York *Herald Tribune* Forum, October 24, 1939, and finished by reading her poem "Underground System," which suggested that the United States was being weakened by those working against democracy, such as Communists and Nazi Bundists. Like millions of other Americans, she gradually abandoned her anti-war attitude and advocated preparedness. After the Germans smashed the Low Countries and France in May and June, 1940, she wrote "There Are No Islands Any More" and threw herself completely into writing propaganda poetry for preparedness and for the cause of the Allies. She was concerned about her husband's relatives in Holland, and her devotion to France and England made her zealous for their cause. She vehemently opposed a third term for President Roosevelt. Her satire "The President with a Candidate's Face" accused him of dictatorial ambitions and of neglecting national defense.[40]

Once the United States declared war, Millay cooperated with the Writers' War Board to produce propaganda, and "The Murder of Lidice" was her chief work of this type. She knew her propaganda-verse was inferior but wrote it as her contribution, even though she feared her reputation as a poet might be destroyed by it. At last the strain of writing propaganda against deadlines and her ill health overcame her. She suffered a nervous breakdown in the summer of 1944 and for a long time was unable to write at all.[41]

Further honors had come to her; but one by one a number of dear friends died during these years: Llewelyn Powys on December 2, 1939; her sister Kathleen and Eugene Saxton, her editor at Harper, in 1943; John Peale Bishop in 1944; and, on November 30, 1945, Arthur Davison Ficke. She must have felt more and more lonely and dependent upon her husband.

VIII *"Long Days Somehow to Be Lived Through"*

The years after 1945 saw some improvement of Millay's health, and she began writing again. She took even more pains than usual to polish her poems because she had grown more critical after her unhappy experience of writing "so much propaganda during the war—from the point of view of poetry, sloppy, garrulous and unintegrated. . . ." By October, 1947, she could assure Cass Canfield that, given time, she would produce another book.

The Boissevains stayed on Ragged Island all summer and late into the fall of 1947. The island summers were periods of isolation, of swimming and sun, of joy and recuperation. Perhaps they did not go to Ragged Island in 1948. They were at Steepletop when Vincent Sheean and Esther Adams visited them on June 3-5, and again during August when Edmund Wilson stopped in one afternoon. Wilson felt that they were living in a sort of backwater of the past; and Max Eastman believed, as does Harrison Dowd, that they were ill-advised to isolate themselves as much as they did.[42]

Nearing seventy, Boissevain continued handling all matters at Steepletop. On August 22, 1949, he wrote in a note to Gustav Davidson: "I have been terribly busy, too busy with haying with insufficient help, to attend to my correspondence."[43] Eight days later he was dead. According to the *New York Times*, he had X-ray examinations in Albany and then entered Deaconess Hospital in Boston, where it was found that he had cancer of the right lung. The lung was removed; he rallied and seemed to be recovering. Then he suffered a stroke and died August 30, 1949.

After his funeral, Millay apparently drank recklessly and did not eat properly. Presently she had to enter Doctors' Hospital. But she was determined to return to Steepletop on September 24, and though friends were opposed to her decision—"Mr. Brann says in two weeks there will be a repetition," wrote Margaret Cuthbert to Mrs. Ficke—Cass Canfield of Harper drove her back home. She was anemic, but with steaks in her deep freeze, other proteins, and vitamins she began a regime of rehabilitation which was soon successful. "If Edna is all right, then she's perfectly businesslike."[44]

Stoically enduring her grief, Millay passed a lonely year at Steepletop. Her professional interests soon reasserted themselves. She was concerned in November with the quality of W. R. Benét's introduction to a new edition of *Second April* and *The Buck in the Snow*; by December 10, she was working on some poems; and on June 23, 1950, she was objecting to the overuse by anthologists of her simple, youthful poems, especially the Shakespearean sonnets. Her later sonnets were nearly all Petrarchan.

She was accumulating more poems and would have had another book. But the volume, when published, was the posthumous *Mine the Harvest*. Vincent died at Steepletop of a heart attack; she was alone, sitting on the stairs, on that night of October 19, 1950.

CHAPTER 4

'All That Once Was I!'

I   Renascence and Other Poems

R ENASCENCE," the most salient poem in Millay's first volume, conveys with extraordinary freshness and with generally fine technique a sense of the immense mystery of the universe.
Like much of her poetry, it is in the tradition of American tran-
scendentalism. "Interim" and "The Suicide" are ambitious pieces
of apprentice work that reflect the encounter of late adolescence
with problems of death, duty, and world-design. Aspects of the
poet's genius later to be much more fully demonstrated are revealed in other poems of the book: the intense, observant wor-
shiper of beauty, and the girl who, in sonnets and brief lyrics,
catches the nuances of feminine loves and sorrows.

"Renascence," (*CP*, 3-13) a substantial work (214 lines) in
tetrameter couplets, falls into four sections. The introductory section (lines 1-28) emphasizes the limitations of the environment
and the desire to reach out to freedom. But for the as yet unde-
veloped soul, the sky itself is "not so grand," only an arm-length
above: "And reaching up my hand to try,/I screamed to feel it
touch the sky." The great identification-experience of the second
section (lines 29-102) is then developed, from the pressing down
of Infinity upon the poet and the holding of a glass before her
"shrinking sight" "Until it seemed I must behold/Immensity made
manifold," through the consequent awareness of the workings of
the Universe and the suffering of all the world's pain and sin, to
the capitulation, death, and sinking into the grave of the "tortured
soul." In the third section (lines 103-80), with the falling of rain
upon the grave, the poet gradually feels again a longing for life
and beauty that is finally voiced in the vehement prayer "O God,
I cried, give me new birth,/And put me back upon the earth!" The

grave is washed away by a torrent of rain, the senses are restored, and the poet is reborn: "I breathed my soul back into me." The fourth and last division (lines 181-214), like the first, is short; it expresses exultant joy in earthly beauty, and even deeper rapture in the new knowledge of God, and the conclusion that the experience justifies: "The world stands out on either side/No wider than the heart is wide;/Above the world is stretched the sky,—/No higher than the soul is high."

"Renascence" opens with simple, little-girl language; then, as Louis Untermeyer wrote: "mystery becomes articulate. It is as if a child playing . . . had, in the midst of prattling, uttered some shining and terrible truth."[1] The terrifying vastness of the universe and the awesome complexity of individual forms issuing from the divine energy—"Immensity made manifold"—are represented in the second part with stimulating, specific words, as in "And brought unmuffled to my ears/The gossiping of friendly spheres,/The creaking of the tented sky,/The ticking of eternity." Such specific terms and metaphors that they imply brought praise of the poem for its remarkable freshness. The imagined situation of the finite human being taking on the omniscience of God is extremely striking. No doubt many people have toyed with this idea: "I saw and heard, and knew at last/The How and Why of all things, past,/And present, and forevermore." But to render the experience with anything like justice in some fifty lines is a large undertaking, and the poet met the challenge.

The reader is made aware of the evil of "the Universe, cleft to the core," through the metaphor of the "great wound" (which evidently is to be imagined as a gash inflicted after a deadly snake bite)—". . . and could not pluck/My lips away till I had drawn/All venom out." Then follows "infinite remorse of soul." Though the poem contains many examples of effective run-on lines, the enjambment is especially fine in the succeeding passage, the stresses falling on the key words:

> All sin was of my sinning, all
> Atoning mine, and mine the gall
> Of all regret. Mine was the weight
> Of every brooded wrong, the hate
> That stood behind each envious thrust,
> Mine every greed, mine every lust.

The passing from the "all" to the "every" is particularly intense, as expressed in examples of death by fire, of starvation, of ship-wreck—when "A thousand screams the heavens smote;/And every scream tore through my throat." Then the poem returns to the general: hurt and death create compassion; but in fact it is the blended elements of godhead, omnisentience plus love, justice, and pity: "All suffering mine, and mine its rod;/Mine, pity like the pity of God—" that prove too much for the "finite Me." For how can one—especially when young, at the threshold of adult years—face such a world? Better to die than to participate in a world so poisoned with suffering and sin. At last the "anguished spirit" is free; the poet sinks into the earth and enjoys the peace of death.

Then upon the silent, lonely grave there falls the "pitying rain": "I lay and heard each pattering hoof/Upon my lowly, thatchèd roof. . . ." And the poet develops greater love for the "friendly sound" of the rain—indeed, for all the "multi-colored, multi-form,/ Belovèd beauty" of earth. All through this section the poet uses alliteration boldly and varies the iambic foot with great vigor and success, especially in relation to run-on lines:

> To drink into my eyes the shine
> Of every slanting silver line,
> To catch the freshened, fragrant breeze
> From drenched and dripping apple-trees
>
> . . . .
>
> Until the world with answering mirth
> Shakes joyously, and each round drop
> Rolls, twinkling, from its grass-blade top.

After the prayer—"And let the heavy rain, down-poured/In one big torrent, set me free—" the answer comes in terms of several implied metaphors: the "rush/Of herald wings," "the vibrant string/Of my ascending prayer," "the startled storm-clouds reared on high"—until at the tremendous climax, the feeling heightened with heavy alliteration, spondaic feet, and assonance, ". . . the big rain in one black wave/Fell from the sky and struck my grave."

After this crashing crescendo and a dramatic pause, the poem resumes *pianissimo*—"I know not how such things can be,"—explaining how the senses of smell, hearing, and feeling return; and then, climactically, comes the sense of sight:

> And all at once the heavy night
> Fell from my eyes and I could see!
> A drenched and dripping apple-tree,
> A last long line of silver rain,
> A sky grown clear and blue again.

The enjambment preceding *fell* gives the word a great force at just the right place; just right, too, are the three lines that follow: each contains a separate observation going from small to large, and each has its distinctive alliteration. With beauty and sweetness, "a miracle/Of orchard-breath," the soul returns.

The joy that follows is emphasized with dramatic inversion: "Ah! Up then from the ground sprang I/And hailed the earth with such a cry/As is not heard save from a man/Who has been dead, and lives again." The Lazarus-ecstasy is quickly modulated to adoration and confidence; the soul reborn is also re-formed, or transformed:

> O God, I cried, no dark disguise
> Can e'er hereafter hide from me
> Thy radiant identity!
> Thou canst not move across the grass
> But my quick eyes will see Thee pass. . . .
>
> .   .   .   .
>
> God, I can push the grass apart
> And lay my finger on Thy heart!

The experience has been apocalyptic. In spite of dark disguises (the evil shot through the world), God is everywhere. The poet's feeling of renewed certainty resembles that of Adam, who, "recall'd/To life prolong'd," was assured by Michael of God's omnipresence: "and of his presence many a signe/Still following thee" (*Paradise Lost*, XI, 330-31, 351-52). The poet concludes from her experience that life is not to be estimated in terms of material environment: the dimensions of one's life are commensurate with heart-breadth (sympathy) and soul-height (spiritual elevation).

Although the poem is in the transcendentalist tradition of Emerson and Whitman, the simplicity and mysticism of "Renascence" made readers think of Blake and Coleridge. Early in his correspondence with Millay, Ficke made inquiries concerning her knowledge of these poets. Though she had read Coleridge, she denied that "Renascence" was written in imitation of "The Ancient Mariner"—"And I never even heard of William Blake. (Should I admit it, I wonder?)" She vigorously asserted her independence: "As to the line you speak of—'Did you get it from a book?' indeed! I'll slap your face. I never get anything from a book. I see things with my own eyes, just as if they were the first eyes that ever saw, and then I set about to tell, as best I can, just what I see."

Harriet Monroe praised "Renascence" highly: "The surprise of youth over the universe, the emotion of youth at encountering inexplicable infinities—that is expressed in this poem, and it is a big thing to express. Moreover, it is expressed with a certain triumphant joy, the very mood of exultant youth; and the poet gets a certain freshness into a measure often stilted."[2] Since the danger of sing-song monotony in iambic tetrameter couplets is notorious, Millay took a considerable risk in using the measure; she invited comparison, for example, with Milton's "L'Allegro" and "Il Penseroso," Marvell, and Emerson. Her work, sensitively varied in rhythm, in enjambment, and in the placing of the caesura, endures the comparison very well.

If "Renascence" owes anything to the example of other poets, they are probably Marvell and Browning. When at Barnard, Millay wrote to Ficke: "You didn't know that Andrew Marvel [sic] is an old love of mine and that his *Coy Mistress* is one of my favorites." Line 116 of "Renascence," "A grave is such a quiet place," inevitably reminds one of Marvell's "The grave's a fine and private place"; and there is something of Marvell's metaphysical tone in lines 29-44. Browning's "Easter-Day" also recounts an apocalyptic experience; the speaker becomes aware of the world on the verge of Judgment-Day—

> . . . the utmost walls
> Of time, about to tumble in
> And end the world—   (XV)

and he boldly chooses the world—

> It was so beautiful, so near
> Thy world. . . .

[74]

> Nor did I refuse
> To look above the transient boon
> Of time; but it was hard so soon
> As in a short life, to give up
> Such beauty: I could put the cup
> Undrained of half its fulness, by;
> But to renounce it utterly,
> —That was too hard!　　　　(XVI)

The feeling resembles that in "Renascence"; Browning's poem differs from Millay's in having a debate between the human speaker and God, who scornfully allows him all the opulence of earth and "its shows." The speaker finally rejects earth, hoping to reach "the Better Land!" "Then did the Form expand, expand—/I knew Him through the dread disguise . . ." (XXXII). The phrasing is reminiscent of Millay's "dark disguise." Browning's poem is also written in tetrameter couplets, and there are some similarities in versification, particularly in Section XV of "Easter-Day." Both poems use iambic tetrameter with a good deal of repetition, alliteration, and enjambment.[3] But "Renascence" is not set up in terms of a contrast between earth and some "Better Land." The basic difference in these poems is that between Victorian orthodoxy and transcendentalist pantheism.

In a few places where Millay's diction falls to triteness, she attempts to set things right by crying out with strained vehemence. Some padding and strain are especially noticeable in lines 49-55, with "would fain pluck . . . nay! . . . Ah, fearful pawn: . . . paid I toll. . . ." She is also betrayed by the *self-elf* rhyme into the fatuousness of lines 161-62: "A sound as of some joyous elf/Singing sweet songs to please himself." Another weakness is what Edward Davison called the "girlish pretty-pretty-ness" of "I 'most could touch it with my hand!" But these are few and minor blemishes in a fine poem which with sense impressions of extraordinary precision ("The creaking of the tented sky,/The ticking of Eternity"); with high metaphorical voltage ("each pattering hoof" of the rain); and with a beautiful matching of sound and sense, communicates reverberantly to the imagination a tremendous yet subtle experience. Untermeyer called it "possibly the most astonishing performance of this generation"; Floyd Dell found it "comparable in its power and vision to 'The Hound of

Heaven' "; and Davison said: "No girl of her age has ever written a better poem."[4]

"Interim" is a blank-verse soliloquy expressing the grief of a man after the recent, unexpected death of his sweetheart; "The Suicide" is a sort of allegorical narrative in heroic couplets. Professor Brewster at Barnard praised the latter for its smooth verse, its "many striking figures," and "great command of language"; but Witter Bynner was perhaps closer to the critical mark in saying that he "would gladly dispense with the two long, rather callow poems, Interim and The Suicide."[5]

"Interim" contains some musings about the mystery of God's purposes, a rebellious interlude—"You were my song!/Now, now, let discord scream! You were my flower!/Now let the world grow weeds!" (CP, 21)—a refusal to indulge in conventional outpourings of grief or consolatory belief in immortality of the soul, and a final tribute to faith: "Faith, it is/That keeps the world alive." Without faith no purpose would be achieved; ". . . and the all-governing reins/Would tangle in the frantic hands of God/And the worlds gallop headlong to destruction!" (CP, 23). This figure is followed by similes reminiscent of the experience described in "Renascence":

> . . . this breathlessness of sudden sight
> In which I see the universe unrolled
> Before me like a scroll and read thereon
> Chaos and Doom, where helpless planets whirl
> Dizzily round and round and round and round,
> Like tops across a table, gathering speed
> With every spin, to waver on the edge
> One instant—looking over—and the next
> To shudder and lurch forward out of sight! (CP, 23-24)

The speaker, evidently a "modern" young man, is, like Millay, a free-thinker determined to be honest; but the poem seems both derivative and inconclusive. It reminds one of dramatic monologues of Browning or Tennyson and, as Untermeyer said, "wanders off into periods of reflection and rhetoric."[6]

"The Suicide" is something like Tennyson's "The Palace of Art," though more Pre-Raphaelite in tone. The speaker curses Life because of the work, suffering, and deprivation it has inflicted upon him, though "I asked of thee no favour save this one:/That thou wouldst leave me playing in the sun!" (*CP*, 26). He approaches a strange and ugly door of the house of life, under which, as he nears it, he feels "the chill/Of acid wind"; and "marking the morning hour,/Bayed the deep-throated bell within the tower!" he leaves and goes to his Father's house. There he has joy and no responsibility but finally, "weary of . . . lonely ease," begs for "a little task/To dignify my days." But the Father "shook His head;/ 'Thou hadst thy task, and laidst it by,' He said" (*CP*, 31). Both of these poems lack the dazzling freshness, rapture, and beauty of "Renascence."

Of the shorter pieces in *Renascence and Other Poems*, practically all of which were written during Millay's college years, "God's World" conveys that rapture best and is the most impressive. It may seem old-fashioned with its use of the pathetic fallacy—the woods "that ache and sag/And all but cry with colour!" —and its *thee*'s and *thy*'s and *prithee*; but, after all, it is a formal address which ends with a prayer. More than any other poem, perhaps, it is characteristic of the electric personality supercharged with sensitivity that has been described by so many who knew Millay: "My soul is all but out of me,—let fall/No burning leaf; prithee, let no bird call" (*CP*, 32). The terms used—*crush, lift, cannot get thee close enough, such a passion*—suggest a sublimation of sexual feeling. Her expression of this feeling, as Miss Petitt says, "took the freedom usually associated with masculine creativity. In this respect she, as woman poet, was new."[7]

Millay deals with love in the usual sense in poems of the broken heart, such as "Ashes of Life," which suggests the frustrations of the rejected woman and hints at rebellion:

> Love has gone and left me,—and the neighbours knock and borrow,
> And life goes on forever like the gnawing of a mouse,—
> And tomorrow and tomorrow and tomorrow and tomorrow
> There's this little street and this little house. (*CP*, 36)

Daring to use Shakespeare's *tomorrow*'s (and one more), the poet intensifies the sense of the petty pace that the woman sees herself enduring futilely ever after. In "Three Songs of Shattering," heart-

break is given symbolic expression through nature; the third song
begins:

> All the dog-wood blossoms are underneath the tree!
>> Ere spring was going—ah, spring is gone!
> And there comes no summer to the likes of you and me,—
>> Blossom time is early, but no fruit sets on. (*CP*, 42)

"Indifference," on the other hand, ironically reveals the passion
that cannot be restrained by conventional propriety: a girl self-
assuredly declares she will not leave her bed to take laggard Love
in—though some would even "take him in with tears!" But she lay
sleepless, "And he found me at my window with my big cloak
on,/ All sorry with the tears some folks might weep!" (*CP*, 45).
Rhythmically these poems follow the example of Yeats in "The
Lake Isle of Innisfree," with their four-beat lines in duple rhythm;
and the ballad-like pieces—"Tavern," "The Shroud," "The Dream,"
and "When the Year Grows Old"—suggest early Yeats, though
transposed to a feminine key.

"Sorrow," like "Renascence," deals with the impact of pain upon
the pitying heart. The second stanza shows a fine handling of
trochaic meter and excellently managed verse-movement in the
closing lines:

> People dress and go to town;
>> I sit in my chair.
> All my thoughts are slow and brown:
> Standing up or sitting down
> Little matters, or what gown
>> Or what shoes I wear. (*CP*, 34)

In "Witch-Wife," a lyric of three ballad stanzas, a husband describes an uncanny woman who "learned . . . her mouth on a
valentine" and whose "voice is a string of coloured beads,/Or
steps leading into the sea." He concludes that ". . . she never will
be all mine" (*CP*, 46). This resistance to possession, this suggestion of the flight motif, appears frequently in her poetry. "Bluebeard," one of the six sonnets in *Renascence and Other Poems*,
expresses Millay's woman-independence allusively even though it
is a dramatic monologue by a man who forbade the opening of
one door—behind which lies only

> An empty room, cobwebbed and comfortless.
> Yet this alone out of my life I kept
> Unto myself, lest any know me quite;
> And you did so profane me when you crept
> Unto the threshold of this room tonight
> That I must never more behold your face.
> This now is yours. I seek another place. (*CP*, 566)

Millay used the theme of Bluebeard and the forbidden room several times.

Four of the six sonnets in the first volume were in the Petrarchan mode, which she used in nearly half of her published sonnets.[8] Few of these early sonnets are packed with ore; they tend to be verbose, as in "Mindful of you the sodden earth in spring," with its wordy catalogue of nature exhibits, and "Not in this chamber only at my birth," where the need for rhymes induces padding: "I cried, but in strange places, steppe and firth/I have not seen, through alien grief and mirth." Millay told Grace King in 1941 that this sonnet was written because she "was stirred by the outbreak of war in 1914." She called it "the blueprint of my social consciousness,"[9] identifying herself with all suffering humanity—"And never shall one room contain me quite/. . . Child of all mothers, native of the earth." The sestet expresses world-ranging sensibilities offended by the dying of the spirit of brotherhood among mankind: "So is no warmth for me at any fire/Today, when the world's fire has burned so low. . . ." Her attitude is one of regret, "vain desire," and finally a longing "to gather up my little gods and go" (*CP*, 564).

In addition to "Bluebeard" the best sonnets are "Time does not bring relief," another expression of heartbreak, and "If I should learn, in some quite casual way," in which she imagines reading of the death of her lover from another passenger's paper on a subway train, and which cuts quite away from nature to reflect the contemporary New York scene. It is a modern rendering of the concept that a person who has suffered a terrible grief must be stricken mute.[10] Though "raise my eyes and read with greater care/Where to store furs and how to treat the hair" (*CP*, 565) expresses very well the callous, vulgar world oblivious to private griefs, it should not be mistaken for a callous, flippant feeling on the part of the poet.

II A Few Figs from Thistles

One might have thought from the deprecatory remarks of some reviewers about *A Few Figs from Thistles* that the world, the flesh, and the devil had completely taken over Millay's poetic life. They had regarded her as a mystic with "looks commercing with the skies," and now she popped up as an impudent *gamine* sticking out her tongue with terrible irreverence. But *A Few Figs* expressed gospel for the youth of the 1920's, who with "rash, impatient, wild ardor and insolence and cynicism"[11] were snatching at joy in the post-war years. Floyd Dell saw that these poems, which intensified the "Millay legend" of impulse and naughtiness, matched the mood of youth:

> The state of the young mind is individualistic, egocentric, passionately rebellious against authority. If these boys and girls hail Edna St. Vincent Millay as their poet, it is because she seems to be writing about them.
> . . . The newer mood of girlhood, that mood of freedom which is dramatized outwardly by bobbed hair, finds itself pleasantly expressed in this volume. . . .[12]

In fact, Millay captured the allegiance of her generation exactly as J. D. Salinger for much the same reasons captured that of another post-war generation thirty years later. With the wickedly wide-eyed perversity of the "Second Fig," the don't-give-a-damn excitement of beauty and transiency, the intense brief experience all the more intense because—like the famous candle of the "First Fig," it "will not last the night"—Millay threw down the younger-generation challenge to prudence and respectability: "Safe upon the solid rock the ugly houses stand:/Come and see my shining palace built upon the sand" (*CP*, 127).

This "poetry of mischief and light"[13] ranges from "The Penitent" and "She Is Overheard Singing" through "Portrait by a Neighbour" to "Thursday," "To the Not Impossible Him," and the sonnets "Oh, think not I am faithful to a vow!" and "I shall forget you presently, my dear." "The Penitent" tells with the air of a nursery rhyme about an impenitent who archly confesses: ". . . 'One thing there's no getting by—/I've been a wicked girl,' said I;/'But if I can't be sorry, why,/I might as well be glad!'"

"She Is Overheard Singing" scorns good, patient (and dull) men to delight in the challenge of "my true love is false!" The neighbor who draws the "Portrait" is a conventional housewife shocked by the Bohemianism of one who neglects domestic routine to enjoy the best of the sun before doing dishes, "weeds her lazy lettuce/By the light of the moon," and "leaves the clover standing/And the Queen Anne's lace!" (*CP*, 142-43). Bold and unfeminine, no doubt, to conventional minds seemed the Cavalier praise of inconstancy in "Thursday"—an exotic in this child's garden of verse: "And why you come complaining/Is more than I can see./I loved you Wednesday,—yes—but what/Is that to me?" (*CP*, 129). The hinted approval of infidelity and experimentation also appears in "To the Not Impossible Him": "Now it may be, the flower for me/Is this beneath my nose;/How shall I tell, unless I smell/The Carthaginian rose?" (*CP*, 130). This verse, little better than doggerel, is suddenly transmuted to poetry by the triumphantly successful *Carthaginian*, a magnificently heady adjective.

The five sonnets of this volume, all in the Shakespearean mode, are better than those earlier published—fluent, rhythmically varied, and deftly controlled—and in spite of their wit and comparative lightness, they carry a pretty high poetic voltage. "Love, though for this you riddle me with darts" (reminiscent of Donne's "Death, be not proud") boasts of freedom. One should note the scorn of housekeeping and of loss of independence in "unto no querulous care/A fool, and in no temple worshipper!" Yet, as in other of these sonnets, there is an element of paradox: the poet really wishes to be smitten with the golden arrow: "(Now will the god, for blasphemy so brave,/Punish me, surely, with the shaft I crave!)" (*CP*, 568). The final couplets, handled in a way she learned from Shakespeare, are all effective. The "alterable mood" of the woman is insisted upon in all these sonnets: in "I do but ask that you be always fair," only the man's preservation of beauty will insure constancy; for pleading and anger will merely encourage "further vagrancy" and "irremediable flight" (*CP*, 567). These sonnets assume that the woman no less than the man is playing at the love game. Millay's Cavalier air[14] shows best in "Oh, think not I am faithful to a vow!" This has as its basis the romantic ideal: "Faithless am I save to love's self alone." The paradox appears in the sestet and is climaxed in the final couplet:

"So wanton, light and false, my love, are you,/I am most faithless when I most am true" (*CP*, 570).

Behind this poem are the same intentions regarding love—idealistic, free, unpossessive—that were explained in *The Story of a Lover*, by Hutchins Hapgood, which appeared anonymously in 1919:

> I met men and women who, with the energy of poets and idealists, attempted to free themselves from that jealousy which is founded on physical possession. . . . They tried to rid themselves of all pain due to the physical infidelities of their lovers or mistresses!—believing that love is of the soul, and is pure and intense only when freed from the gross superstitions of the past. And one of the gross superstitions seemed to them the almost instinctive belief that a sexual episode or experience with any other except the beloved is of necessity a moral or spiritual infidelity. . . .
>
> They highly demanded that the love relation should be free and independent, that it should be one in which proud and individual equals commune and communicate, and give to each other rich gifts, but make no demands and accept no sacrifices, and claim no tangible possession in the personality of the other. . . . Their voice was that of strenuous and idealistic youth bearing the burden of a general historical disillusionment.
>
> A burden indeed it is! . . . And since men and women are not unlimited, these idealists among them fell frequently and bit the dust of humiliation and despair. Old tradition and old instinct proved stronger than they and, filled with commonplace jealousy, a new pain was added to the old—they were not only crudely and madly jealous but they also hated themselves for being so![15]

Behind what seemed to many to be merely flippant and cynical indulgence, there lay the claim of devotion to the highest ideal, preferable by far to such externalities as vow-words uttered in some church or office. This claim is set forth most beautifully in "Oh, think not I am faithful to a vow!" with its "certain weight of line rhythm,"[16] balancing of terms, and alliteration, bold in the early lines and subtler in the sestet: "And all your charms more changeful than the tide,/Wherefore to be inconstant is no care:/ I have but to continue at your side."

The bantering climax of the sonnets on the love game comes with "I shall forget you presently, my dear," which accepts with utter realism the biological impulses of lovers that lead them to inconstancy and experiment. The voice of cynical experience cuts through hypocrisy to belittle with colloquial phrases any heroic pretenses:

> I would indeed that love were longer-lived,
> And oaths were not so brittle as they are,
> But so it is, and nature has contrived
> To struggle on without a break thus far,—
> Whether or not we find what we are seeking
> Is idle, biologically speaking. (*CP*, 571)

Critics approved some poems of the volume. "Recuerdo," which represented a very sweet fig from a time of thistles, had straightforwardness, honesty of realistic details, and the excitement of young love, fresh and gay; and "Macdougal Street," though sentimental, conveyed realistically the atmosphere of the Village (both of these poems were in the enlarged edition). "The Singing-Woman from the Wood's Edge" brought out in Irish terms of leprechaun and friar the mixture of good and evil, or perhaps austerity and capriciousness, in the author—and in many another. These poems all employ duple meter with a kind of appropriate syncopation.

In retrospect, the belittling of Millay on account of *A Few Figs from Thistles* seems rather foolish. Millay had wit. Should she be censured for using it, any more than should Suckling, Belloc, or Swift for witty and satirical verses? Of course, she was capable of writing more serious poems on a deeper emotional level. Oliver Wendell Holmes wrote "The Ballad of the Oysterman" and "My Aunt" as well as "The Chambered Nautilus." "Build thee more stately mansions" is dignified and perhaps inspiring; but sometimes the soul prefers an efficiency apartment to a mansion.

Figs is a product of the gay and defiant satirist, only one element in her personality, one part of her versatility. Edmund Wilson has commented on how she kept the *Figs* poems apart from her more serious work.[17] The versatility that led her to write them entailed risk, no doubt; but could any reader of the poet's next volume, *Second April*, believe that the publication of *Figs*, however naughty or meretricious some of the poems may have seemed, had in any way diminished the excellence of the new collection?

III   Second April

Second April is distinguished in several respects: it has considerable variety; it stresses the elegiac note and exhibits greater realism than the earlier volumes; its technical achievements are noteworthy, and it shows new metrical experiments. The second April represents a time of saddened, disillusioned maturity, or gradual maturing. Except for "Journey" (published in *Forum* [May, 1913]) the poems were written during 1918-20, the poet's disenchanting New York years. "Journey" is notable for its observation of nature; a few metaphors ("Whip-poor-wills wake and cry,/Drawing the twilight close about their throats"); a Keatsian richness of detail; and the eloquent rhythm of the blank-verse lines toward the end with their heaped-up stresses.

Insistence on the rapture that beauty gives, the shattering power of that rapture, and the poet's sadness that beauty must die are expressed also in "The Death of Autumn," "Wild Swans," and "Assault." The last poem sets forth the idea most directly: "I am waylaid by Beauty. . . ./Oh, savage Beauty, suffer me to pass . . ." (*CP*, 77). There is nothing in her heart, we are told in "Wild Swans," "Nothing to match the flight of wild birds flying." This eight-line poem with its irregular rhyme pattern closes with the plea: "Wild swans, come over the town, come over/The town again, trailing your legs and crying!" (*CP*, 124). A bold metrist made two separate feet of "wild swans" in the first of the two lines just quoted.

The worship of earthly beauty is also the theme of the "devious, supramundane allegory,"[18] "The Blue-Flag in the Bog" (*CP*, 55-65). Earth having been destroyed by fire, God invites the victims to enjoy Heaven; but the narrator—a child—cannot bring herself to leave the familiar home until a sign comes. It is a beautiful blue-flag still unconsumed, which she protects like a little mother until the God of love and light rescues them; and, in consideration of human love for beauty, He agrees that "In some moist and Heavenly place/We will set it out to grow." The poem has obvious similarities to "Renascence"—the childish phrasing and point of view, the rapture over nature—but it has more homeliness. There is a Pre-Raphaelite air about it—an effect like that of the early poetry of D. G. Rossetti and Morris—produced by diction reminiscent of hymns and a Pre-Raphaelite exactitude of detail. On a homely, village level, for the burnt-out family

> Heaven was a neighbour's house,
> Open flung to us, bereft.
>
> . . . .
>
> Yet I wept along the road,
> Wanting my own house instead.

The gardens of earth are "blackened by strange blight"; in contrast,

> On the windless hills of Heaven,
>   That I have no wish to see,
> White, eternal lilies stand,
>   By a lake of ebony.

After this Pre-Raphaelite glimpse of static perfection comes the realization of the awful result of the holocaust:

> But the Earth forevermore
> Is a place where nothing grows,—
> Dawn will come, and no bud break;
> Evening, and no blossom close.

The poem is in trochaic tetrameter throughout, and many stanzas have a fine verse movement. It shows, also, the power of striking metaphor of which Millay was capable—"fare you well, you shuddering day,/With your hands before your face!"—and of the word used with surprising precision, as in "Not a glance brushed over me"; in "And the bottom of the sea/Was as brittle as a bowl"; and in the word *rotted* in stanza 27 (*CP*, 61).

The narrator can think of Heaven only as alien; the blue-flag is the symbol of those things that she truly *knew*; and paradoxically it provides Heaven with the only thing—one that can grow and develop—which can make the static perfection of Heaven habitable by the earth-bound (earth-loving and earth-loyal) human soul.

Allegorically, human desire can triumph; but *Second April* contains many poems of loss, sadness, or stark despair. It occasionally uses with telling effect the familiar appurtenances of everyday life, as in "Alms" and "Lament." "Alms" is an extended metaphor: the heart is a house which the housekeeper tends numbly and mechanically through the winter: "I light the lamp and lay the cloth,/I blow the coals to blaze again;/But it is winter with your love,/The frost is thick upon the pane" (*CP*, 88). Homely details such as caring for plants ("I snap the dead brown from the stem") and feeding sparrows have here an appropriate symbolic value.

"Lament," as Padraic Colum pointed out, "has overpoweringly the sense of things that are handled."[19] A young widow facing an empty future voices her despair while trying to get up courage to raise her two children. The poem is in duple meter:

> Listen, children:
> Your father is dead.
> From his old coats
> I'll make you little jackets;
> I'll make you little trousers
> From his old pants.
> There'll be in his pockets
> Things he used to put there,
> Keys and pennies
> Covered with tobacco. . . . (*CP*, 103)

Though the manner is not Wordsworthian, here is a simplicity that Wordsworth would have approved: a situation from humble life in which "the essential passions of the heart" are poetically revealed.

Equivalent material of nature and landscape, most precisely observed and expressed, is found in "Elegy before Death." Housman and Teasdale may well be in Millay's mind, but the poem need fear no comparisons; of its kind, nothing can be finer. The poet-lover, who is envisioning the death of the beloved, projects her imagination into the future to perceive that situation, in which—though it seems unbelievable—earth's diurnal course will be unchanged and the world's work continue:

> There will be rose and rhododendron
>   When you are dead and underground;
> Still will be heard from white syringas
>   Heavy with bees, a sunny sound;

> Still will the tamaracks be raining
> After the rain has ceased, and still
> Will there be robins in the stubble,
> Grey sheep upon the warm green hill. (*CP*, 69)

Both the vowel music and the management of the consonants are superb here, the *o* in *rose* and *rhododendron*, the long *a*'s and *e*'s; the *d*'s and *s*'s in stanza one; the *st*'s, *t*'s, and *r*'s of stanza two. "Heavy" is exactly right, and "sunny sound" performs the same sort of poetic work as Keats's "beaker full of the warm South." The shaping, constructive personality of the dead man is suggested in stanzas three and four by the ugly or common things that will miss his handling them: the "sullen plough-land," "the may-weed and the pig-weed"—

> These, and perhaps a useless wagon
> Standing beside some tumbled shed.

> Oh, there will pass with your great passing
> Little of beauty not your own,—
> Only the light from common water,
> Only the grace from simple stone!

The beautiful music of "Song of a Second April" is somewhat more reminiscent of Housman, but all the material has been completely translated from Shropshire to New England. The disillusioned poet can take a little heart because, as she says in "Doubt No More That Oberon,"

> . . . in this dourest, sorest
> Age man's eye has looked upon,

> .   .   .   .

> Still the dog-wood dares to raise—

> .   .   .   .

> Ivory bowls that bear no fruit . . . . (*CP*, 102)

And she can assert, too, in "The Bean-Stalk," the pride of the creator of poetry, the "maker." Thus the greatness and the value of the imagination in such a harsh world are stressed. The poet, having "built" the bean-stalk into the sky, tells of the dangerous but exhilarating climb to such heights; earth seems gone, "the little dirty city" nothing but a "whirling guess." The sensations of climbing in a cold wind are excitingly expressed. Finally, the climber asserts (should one say God-like?) equality with the Giant who has created the sky:

> Your broad sky, Giant,
> Is the shelf of a cupboard;
> I make bean-stalks, I'm
> A builder, like yourself,
> But bean-stalks is my trade,
> I couldn't make a shelf,
> Don't know how they're made,
> Now, a bean-stalk is more pliant—
> La, what a climb! (*CP*, 73)

The vivaciousness and boyish brashness of this poem are remarkable. Millay freshened the meter by a device of irregularly spaced rhymes from one to six lines apart—a device of which she evidently became fond since she used it in later work.

A great contrast is seen in "Spring," which opens the volume and is her first venture into free verse. "Beauty is not enough," she announces. April always reveals the renewal of life: "It is apparent that there is no death." But she is thoroughly disillusioned; for

> Life in itself
> Is nothing,
> An empty cup, a flight of uncarpeted stairs.
> It is not enough that yearly, down this hill,
> April
> Comes like an idiot, babbling and strewing flowers. (*CP*, 53)

Dissatisfaction with the city is shown, too, in several poems; New York no longer exhilarates her. In "City Trees" she belittles the "shrieking city air"; and in "Exiled" she says she is "Sick of the city, wanting the sea," being "caught beneath great buildings,/ Stricken with noise, confused with light" (*CP*, 105).

"Elaine" and "To a Poet That Died Young" show Millay's longstanding interest in Tennyson's work; the latter poem with its skillful allusions provides a tribute to the early Tennyson:

> Still, though none should hark again,
> Drones the blue-fly in the pane,
> Thickly crusts the blackest moss,
> Blows the rose its musk across,
> Floats the boat that is forgot
> None the less to Camelot. (*CP*, 91)

Second April also contains two poems of rather impressive length, "Ode to Silence" and "The Poet and His Book." Although Edmund Wilson said the "Ode" was one of the poems of Millay's New York period that most impressed him[20] and although it is composed with great technical skill (Cook called it "superbly musical, rivaling Tennyson"[21]), it has received little acclaim. Bynner called it "mouldy Elizabethan stuff."[22] Strictly speaking, it is not Elizabethan; it is an example of the free ode and reminds one of comparable things in the great ode tradition from Francis Thompson back to Milton.

The "Ode" comes out of the same dissatisfaction with New York as does "Exiled." The poet searches for Silence, sister of the Muses, whom she calls "Beauty veiled from men and Music in a swound." Her shrines are noisy now; she is not to be found on earth or in Hell or in Heaven. Finally, "compassionate Euterpe," the Muse of lyric poetry, appropriately explains that Silence inhabits a province beyond Death or Life, Heaven or Hell, the province of Oblivion; and the poet says she will seek her there. The first three sections of the "Ode" are best; much that follows is over-parenthetical and wordy. One can pick out various fine passages, such as "And cymbals struck on high and strident faces/ Obstreperous in her praise/They neither love nor know . . ." (*CP*, 109). Some other notable lines are in the pastoral tradition, involving flowers:

> There twists the bitter-sweet, the white wisteria
> Fastens its fingers in the strangling wall,
> And the wide crannies quicken with bright weeds;
> There dumbly like a worm all day the white orchid feeds. . . .
> (*CP*, 114)

Finest of all is the superbly satisfying "And will not Silence know/ In the black shade of what obsidian steep/Stiffens the white narcissus numb with sleep?" (*CP*, 110). Maxwell Anderson was probably right, however, in saying that the poem "is an artificial ecstasy; exquisite treatment cannot save it."[23]

"The Poet and His Book" (*CP*, 82-87) is a plea for survival through the continuing life of her poems. The work, all in trochaic meter, has an eight-line stanza with a nicely varied pattern of line-length and rhyme. It has a mixing of "the sense of actual things" with music, characteristic of seventeenth-century poetry, as Padraic Colum observed.[24] This actuality of things is sharply conveyed in stanza five, where the author thinks of the book

> Waiting to be sold
> For a casual penny,
> In a little open case,
> In a street unclean and cluttered,
> Where a heavy mud is spattered
> From the passing drays. . . .

Her imaginative power shines in stanza seven, which combines scientific knowledge with the wittily macabre vision of the actual corpse:

> When these veins are weeds,
> When these hollowed sockets
> Watch the rooty seeds
> Bursting down like rockets,
> And surmise the spring again,
> Or, remote in that black cupboard,
> Watch the pink worms writhing upward
> At the smell of rain. . . .

Also her knowledge of people and her sympathy are revealed in the catalogue of those to whom she appeals. She is especially sensitive to the boys and girls whom she sees in some attic, "By a dripping rafter/Under the discoloured eaves," lifting her book "out of trunks with hingeless covers." To them she makes her final plea for remembrance:

> Flat upon your bellies
> By the webby window lie,
> Where the little flies are crawling,
> Read me, margin me with scrawling,
> Do not let me die!

The last stanza is a defiant assertion paralleling that of the first stanza: only the body can be brought to earth; but the spirit, the essential "I," will survive.

Millay's elegiac note is especially beautiful in her "Memorial to D. C.," the "perfect bits of tenderness"[25] in memory of Dorothy Coleman, a Vassar student who died in 1918. Part five, "Elegy," with its long stanzas in trochaic tetrameter and irregular rhyme-schemes, seems the finest of these "little elegies." In the background is the concept of the conservation of matter: the body will be transmuted into other forms—"will sweetly/Blossom in the air." But the voice will be lost. In stanza two the poet recalls with fine connotative force many sounds; and in stanza three she brings the poem to its restrained and perfect climax where assonance and alliteration are at their best:

> But the music of your talk
> Never shall the chemistry
> Of the secret earth restore.
> All your lovely words are spoken.
> Once the ivory box is broken,
> Beats the golden bird no more.[26] (*CP*, 123)

Second April also contained twelve sonnets; some—already noted—were inspired by Millay's love for Ficke. The first of the twelve, "We talk of taxes, and I call you friend," had been published in the *Dial* of December 28, 1918, with the title "Quanti Dolci Pensier, Quanti Disio."[27] "Well enough we know," Millay says, how passion will overcome the lovers and "how such matters end." But sophistication will not lessen the greatness of the experience; she gives the flattering assurance that they are joined in their glorious but destructive passion by such memorable heroines as Isolde, Guinevere, and Francesca: "Francesca, with the loud surf at her ear,/Lets fall the coloured book upon the floor" (*CP*, 572).

Sonnet six (*CP*, 577) is equally allusive, and numbers three and twelve (*CP*, 574, 583) make some use of classical allusion. On the other hand, number four (*CP*, 575) is rather incongruously contemporary. Nine of the twelve are Petrarchan sonnets with numbers one, two, four, and five in the exacting four-rhyme form. Number ten (*CP*, 581) inveighs in the Shakespearean vein against "unscrupulous Time." Thus the group possesses considerable variety.

Numbers two, three, and eleven are of high quality; but nearly every one of the sonnets has some weakness. In general, the sestets are more successful than the octaves. In number eight, for example, lines 2-3 have the comparatively hackneyed phrases: "This flawless, vital hand, this perfect head,/This body of flame and steel . . . (CP, 579). Yet the sestet is simple, fresh, and affecting. Likewise, in sonnet twelve, as Padraic Colum remarked, the octave "is deficient in that clear persuasiveness that is surely needed for a sonnet's opening":[28]

> Cherish you then the hope I shall forget
> At length, my lord, Pieria?—put away
> For your so passing sake, this mouth of clay,
> These mortal bones against my body set,
> For all the puny fever and frail sweat
> Of human love,—renounce for these, I say,
> The Singing Mountain's memory . . .? (CP, 583)

The sonnet seems to say, "Shall I put away this mouth of clay and these mortal bones for your sake, my lord? Shall I put away these mortal bones for the fever and sweat of human love?" But surely the sestet implies quite a different idea: "Shall I put away Pieria for your sake?" "This mouth" and "these mortal bones" are those of "my lord." They are not grammatically in apposition with "lord" but with "your so passing sake," taken to represent "lord." Such appositional looseness is to be found from time to time in Millay. She wrote with the copiousness of an Elizabethan; and her rich and copious flow occasionally betrayed her. *Second April* was, nevertheless, a considerable achievement, which put her, O. W. Firkins said, "among the vivid possibilities"[29] of becoming one of the great American poets of the twentieth century.

CHAPTER 5

'Bean-Stalks Is My Trade'

WRITING DRAMA appealed to Millay. She completed six plays, three in a play-writing course at Vassar, two on commission, and one—her most experimental achievement, the famous *Aria da Capo*—for the Playwrights' Theatre. Even the Vassar apprentice work is written with considerable skill. In most of the plays the themes of honor and integrity predominate, along with romantic ideals of love and friendship.

I The Princess Marries the Page

The Princess Marries the Page, her earliest attempt at play-writing, she had begun several years before taking the course.[1] A romantic work, the play has professional, realistic stage directions; but its atmosphere is child-like, that of fairy tale. As the play opens, ". . . in a very big chair, reading a very big book, sits the most beautiful Princess you have ever seen" (1). During her spirited conversation with a Page who sits on the window ledge, it is obvious that they are attracted to each other. The plot of the play is one of pursuit and protection. To find and capture the Page, there come in turn the Chancellor, the guard, and the King himself. While the Page hides in the ivy outside the tower, the Princess tells the Chancellor that he has not been *in* the tower. She faces a harder test with the soldiers, for she has learned that the Page is the son of the neighboring "Sullen King" and is presumably a spy. But she deceives the guard and manages temporarily to confuse her father with scoldings and accusations. When put to the ultimate test, she temporizes, lies, and is about to swear on her soul that she has not seen the Page—when he leaps into the room to save her soul. She tells her father that she will not live without the Page; if he is put to death, she will take her life. The evidence against the Page—a Prince, of course, and actually a King, for his father has just died—is cleared up; and he explains to the Princess that he has loved her since she was a child. The play has its fairy-tale ending, though without any embracing and love-making at the close, quite proper when one recalls that the play was first acted by girls. In terms of drama the poet achieves an excellent theatrical effect when the Page (". . . horrified at her terrible perjury and consequent damnation, leaping into the room") cries: "Lied—to shelter such a man!" (39). The characters, however, are chiefly conventional: the father is a dull old man, the Page a lovelorn but spirited youth. The Princess, the sole female character, is a sprightly contrast to the rest.

The play is written in blank verse, with a good proportion of run-on lines. Yet it has a mixture of styles; the author has not attained a firm dramatic voice of her own. An early passage, set off from the main body of the verse and supposed to be from a book the Princess is reading, sounds Tennysonian or Pre-Raphaelite: "So then the maiden came/Clothed all in delicate colours, like a garden,/And very sweet to smell . . . (3). Other passages have a romantic air mainly caught from *A Midsummer Night's Dream*, such as the Page's talk about the fairies. There are numerous other Shakespearean reminiscences such as the King's warning to his daughter (34-35). The tone of later Elizabethan drama, especially that of John Webster, is heard in the Princess's comments on dying (44). In contrast to the Elizabethan and other romantic echoes, the Princess speaks at times in a colloquial manner (21).

Despite its youthful stylistic unsureness, the play is, as the author herself decided years later, "rather pretty."[2] She could justly be proud of lines like these: "What of your sweetheart? Is there not some maiden,/Some golden-headed herder of white geese,/ Some shepherdess, some dark-eyed violet-vendor/That holds you dear?" (10).

II   Two Slatterns and a King

Two Slatterns and a King, the second Vassar play, which Millay called a "Moral Interlude," is a merry, unabashed imitation of a Renaissance interlude written in four-beat couplets. It has something of the tone of John Heywood's interludes as well as the fluency of Chaucer.[3] Chance, the "cunning infidel" (*Three Plays*, 3) who manages the action, is more like Puck of *A Midsummer Night's Dream* than the Vice of a morality play. The point of the little play (scarcely a dozen pages long) is that, through effects of Chance, even a King may be made a laughingstock.

The King suddenly decides to marry. For his bride he wishes "that maid whose kitchen's neatest," and he goes about inspecting kitchens. Influenced by appearances while making his fairy-tale tests, he rejects Tidy, usually a model of neatness, and marries Slut—to his regret. In the mockery of "a King/Though a sublime and awful thing," (*Three Plays*, 3) one senses an anti-authoritarian joy.

III   The Wall of Dominoes

The third Vassar play, *The Wall of Dominoes*, is a prose work with contemporary setting and characters. The action occurs in "a sitting-room in a New York house, artistically and somewhat excitingly furnished . . ."—a smart, up-to-date setting for a play dealing with topics of much concern to the college generation of 1917.[4] One sees that sophistication is attractive—but to what lengths should it be carried, and at what price procured?

The sophisticated protagonist—"a tall and beautiful girl of twenty-four"—explains to a friend that she was in love with a man but told herself that her feeling was just passion and lost him. "After that I didn't much care what I did—most anything to warm me up. I made up my mind . . . that . . . everything I really wanted to do, I would do—and that's what I've been doing ever since." She adds, however: "There were some things I just didn't want to do—without love. . . ."

She analyzes her situation in terms of the wall of dominoes, which gives the play its title. She had smoked alone, then in her room with others, "and then in public places, and if you smoke it's foolish to say that you don't drink, and if you drink a little, it looks as if you were scared to drink a lot. . . ." So she was surrounded, she says, by a wall of dominoes—"and the wind blew! and each one as it fell knocked down the next. . . . A few of my dominoes are still left standing . . . , but soon the wind will blow again,—and when the next one falls there will be nothing between me and destruction." One thing she would never do—wear hats with feathers; this "never" is another of the dominoes of her wall.

The action comes rapidly to its climax. A guest arrives—a married artist who is the man she loved. She invites him to take her out that evening. On returning, he says that he will not take her unless she loves him, but she is reluctant. The man gets her a hat because of the cold. Though the hat has a bird on it, she starts, laughing, to put it on. He is unconvinced that she loves him. Looking at the hat, she wishes she were dead—"I don't love anybody." He leaves, she weeps; then she says, "I guess I'd better put that hat back where it came from."

The play shows the author's interest in "daring" subjects: the problems involved in living for the moment and doing merely as one pleases, and the dangers of removing all restraints. It is characteristic of the time and focuses on the problems of a bachelor girl in New York. Patton relates *The Wall of Dominoes*, in manner, to *Good Gracious, Annabelle*, by Clair Kummer, a Broadway success of 1916. As he says, however, it is more than a farce; the heroine's bitter-sweet victory, her decision to keep to her code of honor by telling the truth at the cost of temporary thrills and of being thought stodgy is a matter of excruciating strain. As in *The Princess Marries the Page*, honor and integrity are most significant values.

This one-acter received first prize in a competition sponsored by the Association of Northern College Magazines and was published in the *Vassar Miscellany Monthly* of May, 1917. Unlike Millay's verse plays, it was never acted. Its realism and its treatment of contemporary manners—light and satirical in the early part—look forward to the Nancy Boyd stories and dialogues, and ultimately to *Conversation at Midnight*.[5]

IV Aria da Capo

Aria da Capo has the concern with mankind that one expects of a morality play. It begins as a harlequinade; the traditional figures of Pierrot and Columbine are sitting at opposite ends of a long table "with a gay black and white cloth, on which is spread a banquet." The table occupies the center of a set with "a merry black and white interior." The two diners seem a frivolous modern pair; yet Columbine is not so frivolous and changeable-fantastic as Pierrot. A literal-minded girl, she offsets his antics: she knows what day of the week it is; she thinks he drinks too much; she hopes that he loves her now and truly. Their conversation— Pierrot always taking the lead—comprises a few satirical comments on extremist movements of the day. Pierrot imagines himself a radical painter splashing on his canvas ". . . six orange bull's-eyes, four green pinwheels,/And one magenta jelly-roll,—the title/As follows: *Woman Taking in Cheese from Fire-Escape*" (*Three Plays*, 19). Then he becomes a pianist imaging Columbine in sound "on a new scale . . ./Without tonality. . . ." The title will be *Uptown Express at Six o'Clock*. Then he repels her, having become a socialist: "I love/Humanity; but I hate people" (20). These facile wisecracks are followed by equally unimpressive jibes at the theatrical world. When Pierrot becomes the manager of Columbine the actress and she says that she can't act, he replies:

> What's that to do with the price of furs?—You're blonde,
> Are you not?—you have no education, have you?—
> Can't act! You underrate yourself, my dear!
>
> .   .   .   .
>
> I'll teach you how to cry, and how to die,
> And other little tricks; and the house will love you.
> You'll be a star by five o'clock. . . . (21)

Their foolery is suddenly interrupted by Cothurnus, the Masque of Tragedy, who insists on playing his scene. The bored young couple leave, after a bit of futile protest. Cothurnus calls out two simple shepherds, Thyrsis and Corydon, and holds the prompt-book for them. They had not expected to play their scene so soon and believe it inappropriate to do so in a farce-setting: "Our scene requires a wall; we cannot build/A wall of tissue-paper!" Cothurnus, with stern dignity but "quite without feeling, as if he had said the same words many times before,"[6] says, "One wall is like another. . . . Play the play!" (25-26).

The shepherds indulge in pleasant pastoral comment about their sheep, and Corydon suggests that they make a song. Thyrsis wishes to agree but is prompted by Cothurnus to deliver the lines in Cothurnus' book: "I know a game worth two of that!/Let's gather rocks, and build a wall between us;/And say that over there belongs to me,/And over here to you!" (27). They weave their wall with colored crepe paper ribbons. Thyrsis soon thinks it "a silly game" and prefers to make the song Corydon had suggested. Corydon has to be prompted to declare: "How do I know this isn't a trick/To get upon my land?" (28); but, since he insists upon viewing Thyrsis's idea with suspicion, their separation continues. Then Corydon notices that ". . . all the water/Is on your side of the wall, and the sheep are thirsty./I hadn't thought of that" (29). Thyrsis retaliates by being stubborn and selfish. Anger and suspicion increase. Yet for the time—since, as Corydon says,

> it's only
> A game, you know . . .
>   . . . a pretty serious game
> It's getting to be, when one of us is willing
> To let the sheep go thirsty for the sake of it— (30)

they are able to keep their heads and proceed to "reach out their arms to each other across the wall," until Cothurnus forces Thyrsis to express suspicion again. Now Corydon feels that the wall between them has turned his comrade into a stranger, and Thyrsis's invitation to bring the sheep over for water makes Corydon suspect his sincerity. Columbine reappears for an instant to get her hat, and her comment—"Really, you know, you two/Are awfully funny!" (32)—has a pathetically ironic, ironically sinister implication.

Presently Corydon discovers jewels on his land and makes Thyrsis envious. Thyrsis fails to find jewels but comes upon the root of a black weed. When Corydon becomes thirsty, they strike a bargain: a bowl of jewels for a bowl of water. Each is greedy and treacherous: Thyrsis has poisoned the water with the black root, and Corydon has "necklaces" ready to strangle Thyrsis so that he can regain his jewels. He threatens Thyrsis: "For every drop you spill I'll have a stone back/Out of this chain (40). Thyrsis's measured, stony reply is ominous: "I shall not spill a drop." The strangling and the poisoning proceed simultaneously. Thyrsis dies. Corydon, blind and numbed with deadly cold, stumbles and gropes, muttering incoherently, intending to come over the wall—"I want to be near you." Finally he "strides through the frail papers . . . without knowing it" (41). Begging for a bit of his fellow's cloak, he falls upon Thyrsis's body and dies as he draws a corner of the cloak over his shoulders.

After a pause just long enough for mingled pity and indignation to take effect on the audience, Cothurnus "closes the prompt-book with a bang." He leaves, after shoving the table over the bodies, callously "pushing in their feet and hands with his boot" (42), and pulling the cloth so that the bodies can be seen by the audience but not by people on the stage. When Pierrot and Columbine then return, she complains that the set has been disarranged; but Pierrot thinks "it rather diverting/The way it is." She catches sight of the dead bodies and screams. As they examine the corpses, she says, "How curious to strangle him like that,/With colored paper ribbons." Pierrot replies, "Yes, and yet/I dare say he is just as dead." He wants Cothurnus to drag the bodies out; the audience "wouldn't stand for" their eating with the corpses under the table. Off stage Cothurnus advises him to pull the tablecloth down and hide the bodies—"The audience will forget" (43). So the Harlequin characters hide the bodies from the spectators, "then merrily set their bowls back on the table, . . . and begin the play exactly as before. . . . 'Pierrot, a macaroon,—I cannot *live* without a macaroon!' "

Part of the effect of *Aria da Capo* arises from the contrast of the harlequinade and the pastoral—of the frivolous and the serious—neither one close to the "realism" of modern daily life but following ancient dramatic modes. Bored, flighty Pierrot and silly Columbine are set against the shepherds in the abstract dramatic scheme. Each pair, in its own way, represents Mankind—that is, different aspects of the human character. The mad moderns are an updated version of New-Gyse and Now-A-Days in the old morality. Man's workaday character in the world of labor and livelihood is represented by Corydon and Thyrsis—who ought by pastoral tradition to be leading Arcadian lives, but who are, though reluctantly, developing instead separatism, private property, suspicion, selfishness, hatred, cunning, and a will to murder. The pathos is increased by the fact that they are naturally sweet and good; it is not easy for them to learn the "parts" they must "play." Although the death-scene will be played again and again, the young clowns will continue, after only a pause, their blasé love-banter.

Millay's technique allows the juxtaposition of the two differing scenes. It is an expressionistic technique, which, to project the dramatic theme, uses a symbolic playhouse where, fantastically, grotesquely, and allegorically, play is transformed to reality; and those who were "acting" find themselves murdered. What a world —in which the actors who "play the parts" required are killed in dead earnest! The mingling of "illusion" and "reality" accounts for the peculiar impact of the play. One must see things in terms of a circle: an audience of real people in a theater are viewing a play representing a theater where scenes are portrayed by actors who reluctantly take unwelcome "parts" which they find to be "real."

Millay told Grace King that she had conceived the idea of *Aria da Capo* as early as 1916. She had explained the idea to John Reed before he had left for Russia in 1918,[7] and in 1918 Floyd Dell knew she was working on the play.[8] *Aria da Capo* is one of many modern plays in the harlequinade tradition. Patton has identified several with some similarity to Millay's work. Probably the most significant is Robert Emmons Rogers' *Behind a Watteau Picture*, produced at the Greenwich Village Theatre in November, 1917, which combines "real" people with harlequinade characters. After the Poet and the Marquis have killed each other, their bodies are treated roughly: "The Negroes drag the bodies roughly across the grass and dump them into the open grave."[9]

Patton also places *Aria da Capo* in relation to other symbolic, anti-realistic plays of the art theater of the time. Rostand had taken steps in the anti-realistic direction with *Les Romanesques*, in which Millay had played at Vassar. *The Yellow Jacket*, an imitation of Chinese drama by Hazelton and Benrimo, which Millay had thought "altogether ravishing" in 1917, has a "chorus" or "prompter" on the stage during the action, lets the audience see the changing of settings, and uses make-believe stage properties. Cloyd Head's completely stylized *Grotesques*, a verse play of 1915, also had a commentator; symbolic characters, costumes, and settings; and figures of a marionette quality. Millay was familiar with Kreymborg's *Plays for Poet-Mimes*, free-verse plays with stylized setting, characterization, and action.[10] To these one might add Benavente's *Bonds of Interest*, in which the characters are puppets. Millay had played Benavente's Columbine. Finally, Wallace Stevens had used verse in an effective dramatic way in his symbolic one-act play *Three Travelers Watch a Sunrise*, published in *Poetry* in 1916. It is reasonable to think, therefore, that being in the world of the art theater helped Millay to perceive the means by which her concept of the play could be translated into effective dramatic action.

For *Aria da Capo* she used blank verse with only occasional variations. The movement is less formal and regular when Pierrot and Columbine are talking than in the shepherds' dialogue. The inconsequential effect of the harlequinade dialogue is reinforced by the large number of very short grammatical units, the small number of run-on lines, and the colloquial vocabulary (although at times there is just a touch of the archaic-poetic). For example, one finds

> "I cannot *live* without a macaroon!"
> "La, what a woman!—how should I know?
> Pour me some wine: I'll tell you presently."
> "Well, I like that!" "Why, I'll do no such thing!"
> "There isn't a sign of a moon, Pierrot."
>   "Of course not.
> There never was. 'Moon's' just a word to swear by."
> "Well, eat it then,/For Heaven's sake, and stop your silly noise!"
>   (17-23)

The speeches of Pierrot when Cothurnus appears are very colloquial and contrast with the dignified tone of Cothurnus. The shepherds have a larger percentage of longer sentences to speak than have the other characters, and more than forty per cent of their lines are run-on, a proportion twice as great as that in the harlequinade. The beginning of their dialogue about the sheep is serious, dignified, rather lyrical; but during their "game" they speak excitedly, almost like boys. Then when indignation overcomes them, their insinuations of double-dealing are expressed in colloquial language: "I'll say you had an eye out/For lots of little things, my innocent friend,/When I said, 'Let us make a song,' and you said,/'I know a game worth two of that!'" (30). The longer sentences and the run-on lines chiefly set off the shepherds' speeches from the triviality of the harlequinade. As the double killing draws near, the regularity of the iambic meter increases. In sum, Millay varies her verse with appropriate skill in the several parts of the play. Furthermore, whatever suggestions she may have picked up from the example of other dramatists, *Aria da Capo* is a highly original play.

Alexander Woollcott reviewed it soon after it opened. Although he spoke of it as a "fairly enigmatic piece," he advised his readers to see it, for he considered it, aside from limitations of production and performance, "the most beautiful and most interesting play in the English language now to be seen in New York."[11] He regarded it as an anti-war play, and so did most other critics.[12] But "anti-war play" is an inadequate description; Cook came nearer the mark in calling it "a devastating indictment of man's folly, his greed, his quarrels, his war-like games." This broader interpretation is favored also by Patton, who treats the drama as a "telling comment on human treachery and self-betrayal, which often nurture war because they ignore human need and human love."[13] *Aria da Capo* reads a deeper lesson than an anti-war play, for Millay chose to express what is representative and everlasting; the play has more in common with the tales of Cain and Abel and of Everyman than with most twentieth-century anti-war literature.

Aria da Capo is an example of symbolic and expressionistic drama, occupying a position somewhere between the work of Maeterlinck and Wilder. Frank Shay said in 1922 that *Aria* and O'Neill's *Emperor Jones* represented "the high accomplishments of the art theatre in America,"[14] and Millay herself was proud of her play. She wrote in a letter in 1947 that, though it had imperfections (perhaps the commonplace satire on the arts in the first five pages), "it was written for the theatre" and "to see it well played is an unforgettable experience." It has retained unusual popularity for more than forty years: it has often been reprinted, has had many productions, and is still being produced regularly.[15] The high place of *Aria da Capo* in American poetic drama illustrates very well how certain plays "by the use of symbols escape over the boundaries of realism into the evergreen and limitless fields of poetic truth."[16]

V The Lamp and the Bell

The Vassar College Alumnae Association commissioned Millay to write a play for its fiftieth anniversary celebration on June 18, 1921. With her sister Kathleen, she "worked out the idea" of using the fairy tale "Rose White and Rose Red" as the basis of her play; and she finished the play, *The Lamp and the Bell*, by March 18, 1921.

The play is a shrewd practical application of materials to meet the needs of the occasion. Millay had very clear ideas of these needs: "It's written in the first place for Vassar College, in the second place it's written to be played out of doors, as spectacularly as possible, & in a foreign country & medieval times because in that way you can use more brilliant costumes. . . ." She saw very clearly, too, shortcomings of her work, which she perhaps exaggerated:

> . . . in the third place I haven't had time to work it over at all, in the fourth place it's full of anachronisms which I haven't had time to look up & put right, & in the fifth place it's a frank shameless imitation of the Elizabethan dramas, in style, conversation & everything, & of course does not show up so darn well in comparison.—You'll think from all this that it's a bum play. You're wrong. —I expect the darned thing to make a great hit.—There is a lot of fine stuff in it, too,—but some pretty ragged spots.

Millay was acutely aware of the difference between such an imitative costume drama as this one and experimental works like *Aria da Capo* and others favored by the Provincetown. She cautioned Norma not to let any Provincetown Players read it: "they would hate it, & make fun of it, & old Djuna Barnes would rag you about it, hoping it would get to me."

The play opens in a workmanlike way. A brief conversational prologue makes the reader aware of the situation: a widower king with a young daughter is marrying a woman with a daughter; the two girls are to grow up as playmates and friends. The systematic exposition of Act I introduces the characters and the situation at the court of Fiori four years after the king's remarriage. The characters are Fidelio the Jester, a melancholy wit and lutanist; Bianca, the Queen's sweet daughter; Beatrice, "Rose Red," the bolder, more independent daughter of the King; Francesca, a girl in love with Guido, illegitimate nephew to the King. Guido argues with Fidelio, has no ear for music, and seems heavy and ill-tempered.

The two girls have developed a passionate devotion for each

other. It is Bianca who raises the crucial question of who will marry first and whether they will always remain friends. Beatrice's superior strength is shown; she is tender and protective toward Bianca. The nature of the Queen and the King remains to be revealed. Queen Octavia, like the traditional stepmother, is sharp-natured while the King is rational and tolerant. She thinks it not good for two girls to be so much together; the King considers it natural. Yet he allows her to send Bianca away.

Four months later Beatrice and visiting King Mario are falling in love with each other—while Guido bitterly watches them, her hatred of him drawing him to her. Francesca still loves Guido but he no longer cares for her. Vigorous Beatrice, rather a tomboy, resembles Rosalind of *As You Like It*. Guido tells the Queen that she had better get her daughter home so that Bianca, with her attractive weakness, may marry a king. He, of course, desires to prevent Beatrice's marriage, and he has judged Octavia's ambition well, for she has already summoned Bianca.

Act III opens in the following summer. A bridal song is being sung; the courtiers and ladies, grumbling and joking, bring flowers. The first scene is mainly spectacle and song. Bianca, the bride-to-be, asks Beatrice her opinion of Mario. There is sharp irony here, for in reply to Bianca's comment—"I could not bear/ To wed a man that was displeasing to you"—Beatrice assures her: "You could not find/In Christendom a man would please me more" (*Three Plays*, 93). They are still devoted friends, and Bianca vows never to forget Beatrice: "You are a burning lamp to me, a flame/The wind cannot blow out, and I shall hold you/ High in my hand against whatever darkness." Beatrice replies: "You are to me a silver bell in a tower,/And when it rings I know I am near home" (95).

Beatrice, a generous and understanding young woman, does not blame Mario for having given his love to Bianca—"Because you loved me once a little and now/Love somebody else much more. The going of love/Is no less honest than the coming of it./ It is a human thing" (96). One now finds out that, ironically, before Beatrice could tell Bianca of her romance with Mario, Bianca by her first words on her return showed that she loved him; she had already seen him. Beatrice gave up her own hopes, but could be happy in the love of her friend. Mario honors her for courage and nobility, but he loves Bianca for her gentleness. He wishes to shelter her, but Beatrice needs no shelter.

Another great spectacle follows—a wedding dance, during which the King dies. When the court discover his death, the people are confused. (The dramaturgy is rather crude and hurried here.) Bianca can also be noble; on her wedding night she sends Mario away so that she may be with her friend in her sorrow—a situation reminiscent of Portia on her bridal day.

Five years elapse between Acts III and IV. In a market scene, one learns that Queen Beatrice has been injured while hunting— and that King Mario is dead. Later the widowed Bianca is taunted by her mother; why has Beatrice not come to her? Bianca is sure there must be a good reason, but her mother insists that Beatrice had loved Mario. Bianca will not believe it. She goes to visit Beatrice—to "let her lay her quiet on my heart" (123).

When Bianca arrives, Beatrice explains that she has been ill, but asks her to leave; though she still loves her, she has wronged her. Thinking of what her mother said, Bianca asks, "Then is it true?" With relief, Beatrice says, "Yes"; then, mistaking the point of their talk, she tells how, after being wounded by brigands, she thrust at a rider—and killed Mario! Bianca rushes off, and Beatrice "falls unconscious to the floor" (128).

The final test of friendship comes two years later, with Act V, which opens with forebodings. Guido is plotting to take the throne. He still desires Beatrice, and Francesca loves him still. Upon hearing that Bianca is dying, Beatrice starts away but is seized by soldiers. Guido will let her go to Bianca only on condition that she give herself to him upon returning. She finally agrees:

> I wonder now that even for a moment
> I held myself so dear! When for her sake
> All things are little things!—This foolish body,
> This body is not I! There is no I,
> Saving the need I have to go to her! (141)

Bianca, fearing she may die before her friend comes, leaves a message: her two children are Beatrice's—and "all's well 'twixt her and me" (142). Soon Beatrice enters, leaps to the bed—and Bianca, throwing her arms about her neck, dies.

Integrity has been saved and friendship vindicated; and the

good queen receives further recompense. Fidelio announces that Guido is dead, stabbed in the back, and Francesca drowned, "Who last was seen a-listening like a ghost/At the door of the dungeon" (145). Also, the people of Fiori rose up and swept away Guido's men. A further hopeful note is heard. After receiving Bianca's message, Beatrice says "slowly and with great content":

> She is returned
> From her long silence, and rings out above me
> Like a silver bell!—Let us go back, Fidelio,
> And gather up the fallen stones, and build us
> Another tower. (147)

The Lamp and the Bell, with its five acts, was Millay's most ambitious early dramatic undertaking; her prior plays had only one act. It was skillfully contrived for the occasion. The cast was made large by creating, besides the members of the Court, the strolling players of the pantomime and the villagers of Fiori. Spectacle and music are prominent, especially in II.ii, the pantomime scene; III.i, the flower-gathering scene; III.iv, the wedding dance; and IV.i, the Fiori market scene.

Millay thought the play well constructed. Patton points out that the construction involves two triangles, each with two women and a man: (1) Francesca-Guido-Beatrice and (2) Beatrice-Mario-Bianca. In both triangles the rejected woman kills the man, but one killing occurs by accident, the other for revenge. Suspense is well achieved regarding two important questions: Whose wedding is being prepared for? Who killed Mario? As Millay indicated, many elements of the play come from the Elizabethan drama.[17]

The dialogue has a certain amount of wit; the diction is pleasantly simple and natural; the verse is well managed and more homogeneous and more original than that of *The Princess Marries the Page*. But, as Millay wrote in 1947, it "seldom rises above the merely competent." The play has elements of pathos and irony, yet the tragic effect is weakened by the pageant-like succession of scenes spread out over an action covering more than a dozen years and by some dependence on the spectacular and melodramatic. Guido seems a pasteboard villain, and the end is too patly contrived.[18] Nevertheless, ideals of unselfish love and friendship are warmly but unsentimentally revealed at the core of the play.

VI The King's Henchman

The King's Henchman, Millay's opera libretto, is a story of divided loyalties, of love versus honor. King Eadgar of the West Saxons sends his foster-brother Aethelwold to Devon to assess the suitability of Aelfrida, daughter of the Thane of Devon, for the queenship. If she is suitable, he is to woo and win her for the King. A doughty young warrior, Aethelwold is completely devoted to Eadgar, has saved his life from a wild boar, and is not interested in women: "He shunneth a fair maid/As she were a foul-marten" (17). He is praised for his loyalty: people say he will bring the King's "shilling," his betrothed, safely back and will not "spend his nights a-shining of it on his own sleeve" (17-18). Aethelwold is loath to go on the King's errand, for "So many dry leaves in a ditch they are to me,/The whispering girls . . ." (26). But the King, a widower, wishes to marry again and prefers to send a trusty man who is not easily impressed.

This material, the exposition of the play, is brought out in the closing hours of a banquet for which Millay created an excellently jocular and convivial atmosphere. Especially effective are the account of the brothers and the boar, and the vigorous chorus "Oh, Caesar, great wert thou!"

Act II takes place on All Hallows' Eve in a misty forest of Devonshire where Aethelwold and Maccus, warrior-servant and harper, have lost their way. While Maccus searches for their men, Aethelwold sleeps. There beautiful Aelfrida comes to "seek in spell and rune . . ./Her lover that is to be" (49). Seeing Aethelwold asleep, she loses her heart to him; and, as soon as he wakes and sees her, he is smitten. Aethelwold betrays his brother, sending Maccus back to report that the daughter of the Thane of Devon is "nothing fair," unfit for the King—but that he himself will remain and marry her because her father is rich.

Act III reveals the married couple the following spring. Aethelwold is unhappy because of his guilt and his separation from warrior's work, yet still "love's churl" (85); Aelfrida is testily preoccupied with her father's household, sick of living at home with a mind "full of thimbles and churns" (86). She is impatient for her husband to take her to the Court at Winchester where she would enjoy prestige and a fine house. He, of course, cannot take her there. When he tempts her to go to Ghent in Flanders to buy new clothes, she is enthusiastic. He, too, is eager to leave England, though regretful when he thinks of bidding farewell to its heaths and downs. Hope of happier times and places excites them as they sing: "Oh, let us wander far! Oh, let us live forever!/The world is wide, and we are hale, and we are young!" (98).

At this moment, Maccus arrives to announce that the King is approaching—simply to pay his brother a visit. Aethelwold sees three riders coming: the King, and Shame, and Doom. Trying to make Aelfrida understand his danger, he—imprudently—tells her how he came as the King's henchman to woo her for the King and how he lied and betrayed his brother. She is tempted by the thought of the lost queenship. But he angrily requests her, in the name of their love, to remain in her bower disguised as an ugly woman; and she agrees to do it—then is persuaded by her woman Ase not to, in order to "drop thy silver shell, to pick up the gold one" (111).

The King is cordial to Aethelwold, sympathetic for his having wed "a maid no other man would have . . ."(118). Aethelwold suffers, for his sin and for thinking of riding with Eadgar into Wales to fight again; and Eadgar sees that all is not well with him. When the King goes to visit his brother's wife, who he is told is ailing in her bower, Aelfrida steps out, richly dressed and "amazingly beautiful" (123). Eadgar realizes the truth—is bewildered, saddened. . . . Whom, in his whole kingdom, can he trust, if Aethelwold is false? In bitterness, shame, despair, Aethelwold slays himself. All scorn Aelfrida. They sing the Lament for the Untimely Dead: Life goes on, men's many activities, of ax and boat and horse—"and thou liest here." The play ends with a Chorus of People:

> Woe—lo—woe!
> Hearest thou the wind in the tree?
> He that spoke but now is no longer in the room.
> Forth-faréd is he.

Both author and composer of the opera were praised because they had made no concession by inserting arias that would attract the public. "It is almost incontestable that the lyric drama of Miss

Millay and Mr. Taylor is the greatest American opera so far.
. . ."[19] However, Millay's diction troubled some critics. In the interest of authenticity she had used a strongly Saxon vocabulary, limiting herself to words some form of which was in use before the Norman Conquest. To do this seemed to some no more than a stunt in archaism or, as Lee Simonson wrote, "the verbal masquerade of a poetess in a farthingale." He objected to the "vocal brambles" of the text and claimed that the opera proved the inferiority of English to Italian and French for singing.[20] Such objections were authoritatively answered by Edward Johnson, the tenor who sang the part of Aethelwold. He commended its "beautiful English libretto, . . . singable, and soft and welcome to the ear," its lack of triteness and banality, and also its sense of reality and psychological accuracy.[21]

There is much to commend in *The King's Henchman*. The contrasting characters of the brothers and the objectionable quality of Aelfrida are excellently revealed. Skillful dramaturgy created the theatrical entrance of Aelfrida at the door of her bower, the suicide of Aethelwold rather than his death at Eadgar's hands as in the source, and Maccus's fierce bidding of Aelfrida to stand back from Aethelwold's body. The atmosphere of each act is consistently established: the masculinity of Act I, the other-worldly lyricism of Act II, and the mixture of romance and irritable domesticity in Act III. The verse is varied with remarkable skill, from the opening in "Old English" alliterative measures, through the strongly rhythmic choruses, the discursive passages expressing the purposes and moods of the characters, and the love-duet with its fluctuations of line-length and rhyme, to the stark lament at the close. The drama has a directness and simplicity of plot suitable to opera; and the poetry, though naturally not so intense as Millay's lyrics, abounds in imagery. The diction is prevailingly concrete; the style, frequently natural and colloquial.[22]

Although Millay gave the enchanting power of love its full due, the main focus of the play, as Patton emphasizes (169-71), is upon the integrity of the self. When Aethelwold violates his code of honor, betraying himself as well as his brother, his act leads to further betrayal: his deception opens the way for the selfish greed of Aelfrida. In his anguished crisis of realization, his only means of redemption is to drive his sword through his own heart.

CHAPTER *6*

'The Rich and Varied Voices'

I The Harp-Weaver and Other Poems

A S IN *Second April*, many of the poems in *The Harp-Weaver* are written in a mood of disillusionment, grief, or resignation; every spring must be followed by autumn, the beautiful "Autumn Chant" reminds us: "Far and wide the ladders/Lean among the fruit" (*CP*, 152). And with its pictorial, symbolic and philosophical elements, the poem expresses the theme of beauty rising from the dust to which it must return. Human life is assailed with hardship ("Scrub"), death ("Siege"), and misunderstanding ("Hyacinth").

Yet the author finds reward in the "meagre shapes of earth," the bitterness of reality symbolized by "the smell of tansy"; for the hungry heart, the "growing heart," needs the fullness of experience for its mature satisfactions. She can appreciate beauty in unusual places and forms—difficult beauty—scorning mere conventional beauty, as Sonnet 20 (*CP*, 603) effectively brings out. Even grief cannot destroy her recognition of beauty—thus "The Wood Road" is a converse of the bitter "Spring" in *Second April*. The poet distrusts ease and wealth which dull desire; if there is "no wine/So wonderful as thirst," it is better to have a hungry heart than a sated one ("Feast," *CP*, 158). "Honest things," plain and simple ways of living, the common lot of man—these are the choices of the author ("The Goose-Girl," *CP*, 161). The spirit of these poems is akin to that of "Renascence" although the tone is different: by moral effort one achieves a victory over the limitations of environment.

Many poems in the volume reveal the various responses of women in love; several of these—accomplished poems in folksong or ballad style—remind the reader of Housman or Hardy. "The Spring and the Fall" contrasts the romance of courtship with the eventual rough familiarity, even cruelty, that "broke my heart, in little ways." The affront to greatness, to idealism, offends Millay most, not the disappearance of love itself: " 'Tis not love's going hurts my days,/But that it went in little ways" (*CP*, 168). In contrast to "The Spring and the Fall," "Keen" praises the early death of the lover: "Blesséd be Death, that cuts in marble/What would have sunk to dust!" (*CP*, 171). "The Pond" is a clear vignette in which the behavior of a girl-suicide is very plausibly sketched, and Edward Davison praised it for its fine restraint.[1]

The poet's sincere, feminine personality speaks out realistically for women, for girls who have desires and experiences unsuspected by their elders, who are dismayed and disgusted by their cramped lives, who insist on being independent. Thus the girl in "Departure" declares: "It's little I care what path I take " (*CP*, 163); then, concealing her feelings, she tells her mother that nothing ails her and that she will make tea. This poem has the feel of a ballad and, with its simple vocabulary, stresses plain and ugly details, such as *rut, weedy rocks, dump, dock, ditch.* (It would, however, be better without the second stanza.) "Humoresque," compressed into two stanzas, ironically contrasts a girl's supposed innocence with her sordid experience of seduction and the murder of her lover. A longer, more contemporary poem is the dramatic monologue "The Concert": "No, I will go alone./I will come back when it's over./Yes, of course I love you./No, it will not be long" (*CP*, 186). The speaker, an independent woman idealizing music and dedicated to it, explains to her jealous, possessive lover, the advantages of attending a concert alone; she can be absorbed in music, the great art, with which the "you and I" would interfere; the impersonal beauty of music is something greater than the "filigree frame" of their love, and it will make her "only a little taller" than before. The poem, mostly in trimeter, makes skillful use of irregular rhymes and assonance.

Several of the sonnets express the spirit, independent and sometimes disillusioned, of the modern woman. Though the lover in Sonnet 1 (*CP*, 584) is "dearer than words on paper"—for a poet, the extreme admission—she anticipates the time when she will again possess the key of her heart. In Sonnet 2 (*CP*, 585) the poet, made to eat the "bitter crust" of unrequited love, declares: "But if I suffer, it is my own affair." Llewellyn Jones placed Millay with Genevieve Taggard, Louise Bogan, and Elinor Wylie "as the younger woman poets of importance" who "unite in presenting a picture of the spiritual situation in America of the young, sensitive, self-conscious woman. . . ."[2] Her situation is illustrated especially by Sonnet 8: "Oh, oh, you will be sorry for that word!/Give back my book and take my kiss instead./Was it my enemy or my friend I heard,/What a big book for such a little head!" (*CP*, 591). The superior woman's disappointment, her exasperation, and her contempt for being thrust (automatically) back into her merely physical role are expressed in such lines as "Oh, I shall love you still, and all of that./I never again shall tell you what I think." She can condescend to conceal herself in traditional femininity but at the sad expense of losing comradely frankness: "I shall be sweet and crafty, soft and sly;/You will not catch me reading any more. . . ." And finally, she anticipates the day, "some sane day," when "I shall be gone, and you may whistle for me."

With cool disdain she separates blood from brain in Sonnet 18, acknowledging that as a woman she has certain needs and is subject to temptations which leave her "once again undone, possessed." But she ends with ironic contempt: "I find this frenzy insufficient reason/For conversation when we meet again" (*CP*, 601). Millay speaks frankly of bodily appetites, which women share with men; but she does not idealize them; she tends to scorn them. Always she thinks in terms of a dichotomy between body and mind or soul.

Various *Harp-Weaver* sonnets celebrate love, generally with sadness or resignation, expecting it not to last. Yet Millay's idealism is not easily destroyed; she can become reconciled to change and loss, even death, as in Sonnet 9; but the "wound that will never heal" is "that a dream can die." Sadness over fickle love combines with her devotion to the seashore in Sonnet 10: love stood only a moment in the lover's eyes—"But I shall find the sullen rocks and skies/Unchanged from what they were when I was young" (*CP*, 593). Nature, though harsh, is at least uniform and predictable.

Maturity has come to Millay, bringing bitterness and pain. In Sonnet 11 (*CP*, 594) she compares herself to a tree in autumn—

"My sky is black with small birds bearing south"—and in Sonnet 19 to a lonely winter tree, its boughs silent, the birds gone. She can speak frankly of bygone loves; but she has only their ghosts to remember, and the memory brings pain: "I cannot say what loves have come and gone,/I only know that summer sang in me/A little while, that in me sings no more" (*CP*, 602).

Sonnets 13-16 deal with disease, despair, and death. According to Floyd Dell,[3] Millay wrote Sonnet 16 after hearing of John Reed's death in 1920 in Soviet Russia. The questions in the first two quatrains of the sonnet are conceits depending on the classical concept of Hades. The praise of Reed as "a heavenly guest,/Assuming earthly garb for love of me" (*CP*, 599), does justice to the acknowledged charm of the laughing, robust journalist. Sonnets 14 and 15 (*CP*, 597-98) deal with illness. The first was published in *Vanity Fair* (June, 1923) under the title "To a Dying Man." It is constructed in terms of a simile: "Your face is like a chamber where a king/Dies of his wounds. . . ." The poem is complicated by actions of the king in the chamber and by thoughts of actions before he was wounded. One cannot avoid a feeling of confusion in the sestet when mention is made of "your eyes" and "your windows"—presumably the eyes of the face like a chamber. "Through your eyes," the reader is told, "you see"

> . . . fronting on your windows hopelessly,
> Black in the noon, the broad estates of Death. (*CP*, 597)

Despite the strain of these conceits, the ending of the sonnet is impressive. Millay dictated Sonnet 13 to Ficke at Croton-on-Hudson on August 20, 1923, when he was helping her during her convalescence. This funeral sonnet, a poem of deep despair, probably represents something of her hopeless feeling in the summer of 1923. The misery of the sad "similar years" is finely expressed through the unifying details of the funeral image, and the poem ends with a death wish: "I would at times the funeral were done/And I abandoned on the ultimate hill" (*CP*, 596).

But for all the sorrow of her life, there is still beauty. The last three sonnets deal with beauty in different ways. Sonnet 20 (*CP*, 603) reminds one of the beauty to be found in fungus and mildew, in oil-filmed ditches, and in logs of scummy, frog-inhabited pools. The poet is disdainful of the "craven faces" too fastidious to endure unconventional, "difficult" beauty. This talk about beauty is another way, one supposes, of asserting her greed for experience. Sonnet 21 brings before one children playing, leaping, and running. The sestet reminds one that death will still these limbs, the laughter, even the breath—but beauty and strength seem immortal: "And yet, before such beauty and such strength,/ Once more, as always when the dance is high,/I am rebuked that I believe in death" (*CP*, 604).

The final sonnet, "Euclid alone has looked on Beauty bare" (*CP*, 605), with its magnificent first and last lines, has its matrix in a kind of Shelleyan Platonism, in an extreme Idealism. The utmost beauty, the pure concept uncontaminated with any physical representation, the perfect pattern that governs every physical manifestation of beauty, is honored in it. The poet who found mathematics her most difficult subject elected to praise conceptual beauty via the author of the *Elements*, Euclid, the famous geometer of whom it has been said: "He created a monument that is as marvelous in its symmetry, inner beauty, and clearness as the Parthenon, but incomparably more complex and more durable."[4] In a letter of September 11, 1920, Millay coupled Bach, "so pure, so relentless and incorruptible," with geometry and her "sonnet to Euclid."

In the octave of the sonnet the poet cites Euclid as the only one who could apprehend intellectual beauty, contrasting him with those who, being unable to free themselves from personal considerations, only "prate of Beauty." The praters about Beauty— the "geese" that "gabble and hiss"—are invited to keep silent, to "lay them prone upon the earth," and to attempt contemplation of the "nothing, intricately drawn nowhere" but in the mind. In the sestet the poet apostrophizes that splendid moment, "O blinding hour, O holy, terrible day," when Euclid first experienced the pure vision. In the last sentence she points out that those who approximate such an experience—"once only and then but far away" —are fortunate. The poem gains tension from the paradox of a nothing drawn nowhere which can be observed; a nothing in "shapes of shifting lineage" can be observed. One supposes that the geometrical concepts are shapes with a shifting lineage because they can be derived logically from whatever postulates the geometer begins with.

In the contrast of geese and heroes (lines 6-7), she may have had in mind Plato's myth of the cave *The Republic*. If so, the geese are like those prisoners underground, chained neck and leg in "dusty bondage," gabbling about glories and honors according to their false notions. The hero (a Euclid) desires to see reality in the "luminous" air of the upper world, which Plato called the world of knowledge. The one who leaves Plato's cave is at first blinded by the sunlight: "O blinding hour, . . ." The words *vision* and *light*, because of their connotations, have both literal and metaphorical meaning. *Anatomized* seems a strange word to apply to light. Light dissected?—analyzed? Perhaps it is anatomized in the sense of mental light, conceptual knowledge, divided into the particular geometrical elements of the theorems.

"Beauty bare" in the first line refers to the beauty of pure intellectual concept; still, it is a personification; and in the twelfth line, divine Beauty is to be seen as a goddess, like a Diana at her bath. Few human beings have heroic encounters with divinities, especially unclothed divinities. Thus the last sentence about the fortunate ones who have heard from a distance the sound of the divinity's footsteps is relevant. So great is the divine power that the time of such a direct encounter would be marked as a "holy, terrible day"; and the power involved in the lesser experience of hearing is suggested by "massive sandal" and "stone."

Millay set herself difficult problems in these sonnets; fifteen of them are in the Petrarchan pattern, eight of these using only four rhymes. Sentence units are usually few; Sonnet 1 contains only one sentence, and the control of the material, since Millay is addicted to involved and parenthetical constructions, becomes a challenge. Sonnet 12 has an interesting flow of rhythm, seven lines being run-on; Sonnet 19 has six run-on lines; Sonnet 20 has seven. In contrast, Sonnet 8 has not a single run-on line; thus its colloquial tone is enhanced, and it becomes very sprightly. The skill with which the poet manipulates sounds in beautiful patterns of alliteration and assonance is remarkable, especially in sonnets 4, 6, 10, 18, 21, and 22.

The Harp-Weaver and Other Poems contains a few poems in free verse, none very impressive. "To One Who Might Have Borne a Message" speaks of a girl "Now two years dead,/Whom I shall always love." The message-bearer must tell her "That I love easily, and pass the time" (*CP*, 189). Millay may have been writing to John Reed, who died in 1920, about Dorothy Coleman, who died in 1918. Two pieces stand apart from the rest of the volume; these are the title-poem and the seventeen "Sonnets from an Ungrafted Tree." The volume was dedicated to Millay's mother, the inspiration of the title-poem;[5] "The Ballad of the Harp-Weaver" is a story of self-sacrifice by a poverty-stricken mother for her son. The child had no clothes, and all through the autumn the weather grew colder, the situation more desperate, with ". . . nothing in the house/But a loaf-end of rye,/And a harp with a woman's head/Nobody will buy" (*CP*, 177). The mother held her son in her lap, chafed his bones to warm him, and made him happy singing; but by the night before Christmas their state was critical. In the night the mother rose and on the strings of the harp wove "wonderful things," magical garments fit for a king's son. In the morning the boy found his mother at the harp,

> And her hands in the harp-strings
> Frozen dead.
> And piled up beside her
> And toppling to the skies,
> Were the clothes of a king's son,
> Just my size. (*CP*, 183-84)

Allegorically implied here are all the sacrifices of Mrs. Millay, who enabled her brilliant daughter to have royal gifts though the family was poor—the beautiful, romantic "garments" of music, poetry, ideas—the clothing of mind and heart, for which the daughter remained ever grateful.

The poem is a skillful mixture of ballad and nursery rhyme. Well organized, its thirty stanzas are divided evenly at the night-before-Christmas point; it uses six stanzas with an extra line to achieve variety and to indicate organization. Perhaps the pathetic subject and the nursery-rhyme tone, however, make it a poem to be enjoyed primarily by women.

In "Sonnets from an Ungrafted Tree" (*CP*, 606-22) Millay relates the experience of "the New England woman" who returns in winter to her dying husband's house to care for him although she has no love for him. The stark directness and the physical and psychological realism of the sequence are notable. The same ob-

servation of details that one finds, for example, in "Souvenir"—
". . . naked blackberry hoops/Dim with purple chalk" (*CP*, 159)
—appears in these sonnets with utmost vividness; the startling precision of the imagery, both visual and auditory, is impressive. Besides the immediate experience of the woman "ungrafted," Millay
reveals, directly and symbolically, something of the woman's character and her past. As a young woman in that house, she had been
blithe; she had wanted beauty and had painted a butter-tub and
planted red geraniums in it. Now their stalks are rotted, and she
cannot imagine a time, even in summer, when constant rain will
not beat down upon the house. She had been betrayed by loneliness and desire into marriage with a commonplace fellow "not
her spirit's mate."

At the end of Sonnet 10 the "oak tree's shadow . . . deep and
black and secret as a well" is an ominous symbol. Her impatience
and lack of judgment have already been implied in Sonnet 3, in
which she picks up wood in the woodshed, "selecting hastily
small sticks of birch,/. . . that instantly will leap/Into a blaze," and
does not think ahead to a day when only big green logs and
"knotty chunks" will remain—"(That day when dust is on the
wood-box floor,/And some old catalogue, and a brown, shriveled
apple core)" (*CP*, 608). As she blows upon the "stubborn coal,"
she is "mindful of like passion hurled in vain/Upon a similar task,
in other days . . ." (Sonnet 4). One may suppose that the husband
failed to respond to her love and that her life became an exercise
in frustration, suppressed desires, and hardening resentment.

She lives a kind of nightmare existence (Sonnet 13) but finds
some consolation in homely routine details of farmhouse work and
in cleaning up the neglected place. At last her ordeal ends, though
there still remains "The stiff disorder of a funeral/Everywhere,
and the hideous industry . . ." (*CP*, 621). She sees the dead man
now as an unfamiliar person; the work ends with this memorable
simile:

> She was as one who enters, sly, and proud,
> To where her husband speaks before a crowd,
> And sees a man she never saw before—
> The man who eats his victuals at her side,
> Small, and absurd, and hers: for once, not hers, unclassified.
>
> (*CP*, 622)

Sister M. Madeleva thought the sonnets of this sequence were "so deeply rooted in New England soil that they might have been done by Robert Frost." In fact, she thought Frost "unquestionably" Millay's teacher.[6] True, the situation might make one think of "The Hill Wife" and "An Old Man's Winter Night"; but Millay's work in its rhythms and in its use of concrete detail is much closer to the honest, direct poetry of the early William Morris; in fact, much of it is implied in Tennyson's "Mariana," which Millay admired. As a sonnet sequence, it is related to Meredith's *Modern Love* and Ficke's *Sonnets of a Portrait Painter*. (These works are in the background of other Millay sonnets too.) According to a note by Ficke on the writing of a preface for *Collected Sonnets*, Millay said in the original preface that Ficke's and Meredith's sonnets "had been the origin of her own use of the sonnet."[7] Meredith used a sixteen-line "sonnet" in *Modern Love*; similarly, Millay took liberties with the sonnet form in "Sonnets from an Ungrafted Tree." She used three quatrains and a couplet, but the third quatrain rhymes *e f f e*, and the fourteenth line has seven feet. The usual Shakespearean content-divisions are ignored in most of the sonnets, which are treated as stanzas, fourteeners.

II The Buck in the Snow

Technically, *The Buck in the Snow* shows a greater range of experimentation than Millay's earlier volumes: nearly half of the shorter lyrics have an irregular verse movement that, at first glance, looks like free verse; but the reader soon discovers blossoms of rhyme starring the lines that the poet, with instinctive sureness, has varied in length. The variety of rhythms is notable: dactylic-anapestic feet are numerous although they do not actually predominate over the iambic-trochaic. In these works—such as "Mist in the Valley," "The Pigeons," "The Buck in the Snow," "Pueblo Pot," and "On First Having Heard the Skylark"—the assured, experienced poet is at the peak of her art.

Representative of her times, Millay embraced the idea of an indifferent universe. In "To the Wife of a Sick Friend," a tribute to Arthur Ficke,[8] she speaks of "the cave wherein we wander lost," which the man-candle illuminates and beautifies "Till a man would rather be lost than found:/We have forgotten where we are" (*CP*, 209). The candle must be sheltered from the wind of death; if it is extinguished, the poet and Mrs. Ficke will be left in "unmitigated dark," "a terrible place." In "Dirge without Music" all fine persons must go 'into the darkness" to "be one with the dull, the indiscriminate dust"; there they will "feed the roses." Millay does not approve of this: "More precious was the light in your eyes than all the roses in the world." Without Christian hope of immortality, she rebelliously sees ahead only the classic pagan darkness. "I am not resigned" (*CP*, 240), she writes.

Optimistic ideas of any sort of immortality she brushes aside as visions—"the grave's derisions"—and she insists that life at its worst is worth contention. In the last ten stanzas she creates a vividly ugly picture of helpless old age, but she declares that even such a life with all its indignities is preferable to death's "nothing good." The last three stanzas assert defiant resistance to the last breath. The sonnet "Not that it matters, not that my heart's cry" (*CP*, 625) also assumes an indifferent, mechanistic universe: only love, like a jewel scratched from a tomb, has force enough to stand out—temporarily—against the victor Death.

Other reasons exist for bitterness and grief. The passing of the sharp sensations of childhood and youth is one: "The Plum Gatherer" (*CP*, 248) expresses her regret that the sweet plums are gone. She would gladly pay a price of pain for them, the customary nettle-stings of childhood—"Anything, anything." But no longer do nettles sting.

Though in "Renascence" she had felt all sin and pain, the Sacco-Vanzetti experience brought directly home to her the bitterness of injustice, the realities of harshness, prejudice, and suffering therefrom—so that she wrote, in "The Anguish": "The anguish of the world is on my tongue./My bowl is filled to the brim with it; there is more than I can eat" (*CP*, 229). Even before the execution she wrote in "Justice Denied in Massachusetts" of the blighted crops—the ruined traditions of justice and free speech—under the cloud of injustice in Massachusetts. To her it seemed a permanent darkening of America: the sun would not appear again—"We shall not feel it again./We shall die in darkness, and be buried in the rain"[9] (*CP*, 231).

"Wine from These Grapes" depends in part for its effect upon the reader's recollection of "trampling out the vintage where the grapes of wrath are stored." It is based on the metaphor of an indelible stain: "Stained with these grapes I shall lie down to die" (*CP*, 234). Evidently the Sacco-Vanzetti affair gave the poet a permanent conviction that the times were out of joint—a feeling of bitter disillusionment, distrust, and alienation. One supposes that the pungent "Sonnet to Gath" and the sonnet "To Jesus on His Birthday" also reflect her disillusionment after the Sacco-Vanzetti affair, although the latter poem bitterly scores the perfunctory frivolity of Christmas. "Nobody listens" to the Christian message: "The stone the angel rolled away with tears/Is back upon your mouth these thousand years" (*CP*, 628).

Yet other poems strongly assert her admiration of daring and hardihood, her conviction that the life-experience is essentially good. The sonnet "Life, were thy pains as are the pains of hell" upholds the value of living, no matter how much suffering is entailed; this utterance is not that of a stoic but, it seems, of an enraptured vitalist to whom the earthly joys are heavenly: "So fair to me thy vineyards, nor less fair/Than the sweet heaven my fathers hoped to gain;/. . . Needs must I gather . . ." (*CP*, 623).

Millay feels, too, that intangibles like love, beauty, magnanimity, and courage have value. Some of the poems reflecting the Steepletop environment show this concept; "The Bobolink" and "The Hawkweed" are examples. She admires the bobolink as an epitome of gallantry and daring, ignoring the precariousness of life; and she loves the bird's defying of adversity, which is exactly to her heart: "Bobolink, you and I, an airy fool and an earthy,/Chuckling under the rain!" (*CP*, 212). Hawkweed is the ploughman's enemy, worthless as food; but, although Millay approves of efforts to mellow the fields and increase their harvest, she balances the need for the practical by a demand for beauty.

The great pictorial qualities of her poetry appear frequently in *The Buck in the Snow*. The title poem reminded Cook of "the soft, the subdued, but fluid movement of a Japanese print. . . ."[10] One who knows Northern winters feels at once that all the details of the picture are exactly right. Millay used her skill to slow up the *l*-crammed line showing the deer leaving the orchard—"Tails up, with long leaps lovely and slow" (*CP*, 228)—to point, by inversion, with deliberate finality at the dying buck, all his intense vitality concentrated in *wild* and *scalding*: "Now lies he here, his wild blood scalding the snow"—and to picture the doe hiding "under the heavy hemlocks," an incarnation of puzzled, precarious life—"Life, looking out attentive from the eyes of the doe."[11] The verse-movement and the alliteration are beautifully controlled. The sense of the chill muffling whiteness is emphasized by ending five of the twelve lines with *snow*.

Another colorful pictorial poem is the imagistic "Pueblo Pot," in which the poet presents the red-shafted flickers, ". . . flashing the wonder of their under-wings; . . ./Wrenching the indigo berry from the shedding woodbine/with strong ebony beak" (*CP*, 250). (The musical line is made emphatic by the vigorous alliteration.) The beauty of the Indian pot destroyed, the birds cannot "solace" it; they replace it with another perfect beauty. The individual manifestations of beauty, impermanent, are often casualties; and the life of physical sensations is transient, like the seasons.

The Buck in the Snow deals as much with the past remembered as with the dramatic present. Acutely aware of transience, Millay writes poems like "The Road to Avrillé," which may commemorate a brief French love affair, and "Song," which states that Summer "is gone again like a jeweled fish from the hand" (*CP*, 208). This muted lyric with a fine pattern of alliteration is one of her most accomplished creations. As the poet reached her middle thirties, she became more involved with her past, with a nostalgic regret for experiences irrevocably gone—save in the memory. The transience of things assailed by devouring time makes more significant both the memories and the maintaining of love and friendship.

The remarkable "Cameo" represents a memory of lovers on a beach—"O troubled forms, O early love unfortunate and hard,/Time has estranged you into a jewel cold and pure . . ." (*CP*, 246). Though the exact words and the pain of the lovers are lost, the incident persists in memory "like a scene cut in cameo." "To a Musician" and "The Pigeons" also deal with the past, but in them the estrangement of time has not been completed. The pigeons are presented onomatopoetically: "How they conversed throughout the afternoon in their monotonous voices never for a moment still." They symbolize the past; but the painter drove them away. The poet visualizes him continuing to paint "in a quiet room, empty of the past, . . . thinking of me no more"; but she, regretful for having left him, must "Walk in a noise of yesterday and of the days before,/Walk in a cloud of wings intolerable, shutting out the sun as if it never had been" (*CP*, 226-27). "Portrait," which is about Edmund Wilson reading to her in Greenwich Village days,[12] is partly based on memories but also touches an immediate present.

The old intensity of her response to life is projected into her remembrance "On First Having Heard the Skylark," when she was overwhelmed by "his sweet crying like a crystal dart" and felt as though "beset by angels in unequal fight, . . ." Then she saw the bird "Above me in the bright air,/A dark articulate atom in the mute enormous blue,/A mortal bird, . . ." (*CP*, 256). And, calling him "Blithe Spirit!," she fell and ". . . lay among the foreign daisies pink and small,/And wept, staining their innocent faces with fast-flowing tears." She wept because, joined with her rapture in the notes, there rushed upon her all her memories of the skylark as the subject of immortal poems. But the implication of the first lines of the poem is that she would not have responded so if she had known then that the lark had "A wing of earth, with the warm loam/Closely acquainted. . . ." The poet's need to keep in touch with earth is brought out in the sonnet "Grow not too high, grow not too far from home." Earth must furnish the sustenance of the tree of poetry; therefore

> Have done with blossoms for a time, be bare;
> Split rock, plunge downward; take heroic soil,—
>
> .   .   .   .
>
> Earth's fiery core alone can feed the bough
> That blooms between Orion and the Plough. (*CP*, 624)

Presumably that starry bough of poetry must be connected with the hot life of struggling and suffering earth. But earth brings to sensitive spirits the spring-raptures of "Northern April" (*CP*, 219), which might be called a "God's World" of a dozen years after. A poem with an original verse-pattern, it suggests the almost unbearable thrill of renewed activity after winter. The repetitions of "quiet," "never for a moment quiet," and "have pity upon us" suggest the nigh-frantic feeling of the winter-paled who "emerge like yellow grass." The poet prays April to relax, to have pity, "till the green come back into the vein, till the giddiness pass."

The volume closes with the Shakespearean sonnet "On Hearing a Symphony of Beethoven," a poem highly praised by Untermeyer —in spite of "its almost fatal first line"—as "that rarest of things, a successful poem on a symphony."[13] The sonnet is a tribute to the power of great music to create an enchanted and perfect world in which the enraptured listener would wish to remain forever. Lines 3 and 4 are exquisitely arranged. From line 5 on Millay has in mind the story of the Sleeping Beauty: "Enchanted in your air benign and shrewd,/With limbs a-sprawl and empty faces pale,/ The spiteful and the stingy and the rude/Sleep like the scullions in the fairy-tale" (*CP*, 629). *Shrewd*, which at first seems puzzling, may be used in its archaic sense of "artful," and thus "magical." In the sestet of the sonnet the poet herself becomes metaphorically the city "spell-bound under the aging sun,/Music my rampart, and my only one." So music—could the wish be granted—would replace the traditional thorn hedge as a defense against an intrusive world of change, uncertainty, and evil.

English reviewers were better pleased with *The Buck in the Snow* than were American critics. The book does not contain novelties regarding the author's personality or thought, but it is more mature, less clever and more thoughtful, than her earlier volumes; and it has much in technical respects that is fresh and interesting.

III Fatal Interview

The sequence of fifty-two Shakespearean sonnets published in April, 1931, as *Fatal Interview*, Millay originally intended to issue under the title *Twice Required*, a phrase from Sonnet 14: "Since of no creature living the last breath/Is twice required. . . ." In fact, a publisher's dummy containing three sonnets was printed with that title. But 1931 was Donne's tercentenary year, and it was decided, according to Norma Millay, to change the title, the epigraph of the volume being taken from Donne's "Elegy 16": "By our first strange and fatall interview,/By all desires which thereof did ensue." The new title was a better one; but it implies no connection between Donne's work and Millay's sonnets.

Fatal Interview presents a woman's responses to a passionate love affair from first attraction through the ecstasies of consummation to the sorrows of breaking-up (because the lover grows cold) and eventually to resignation. Sonnets 1 and 52 deal with the legend of Diana and Endymion, the moon-goddess and the handsome mortal with whom she fell in love. Between these sonnets are fifty others which imply a story and express a woman's feelings as she passes through a love affair which may possibly represent one that actually took place.[14]

It is not likely that in Sonnet 1 the poet would speak of herself or any mortal woman as immune from the doom of mankind and ask: ". . . what thing is this/That hastening headlong to a dusty end/Dare turn upon me these proud eyes of bliss?" The speaker is a goddess. In Sonnet 2, however, no goddess but a woman apparently living in New England, or a place like Steepletop, says: "I shall forget before the flickers mate/Your look that is today my east and west." The eyes of the man are especially distinctive and irresistible; they are mentioned not only in sonnets 1 and 2 but also in 4 ("eyed with stars") and 9 ("disturbing eyes. . . . remembered morning stars"). In sonnets 2 to 5, inclusively, love is represented as a disease ("the sick disorder in my flesh"—Sonnet 4) which she cannot conceal.

With Sonnet 6 there is a sudden shift, and she blames the man for ignoring her on account of his "pale preoccupation with the dead" heroines of old love stories. It is hard to tell whether this sonnet is a dramatic monologue or a soliloquy, but in any case it expresses her impatience with the oblivious, unresponsive man. He alone could save her from being drowned in love (Sonnet 7), but she does not expect him to. Her mood shifts then from self-pity to scornful accusation as she warns him how short life is. But she cannot free herself from loving and, against her own philosophy of freedom, is driven to possessiveness. The reader is to suppose that her sweet and guileless offer of "love in the open hand" (Sonnet 11) wins him at last, for Sonnet 12 expresses the raptures of consummation. She is a mortal woman whose bed Zeus himself has honored ("Enraptured in his great embrace I lie"), and she foresees having a demigod for a son.

The next eight sonnets present her shifting moods: hatred of separation, insatiable desire, foreboding that love will betray her, praise of the lover, first regrets, the repulsion-fascination of being love's helpless prisoner and finally, in Sonnet 20, rebellion again against possessiveness. It is not clear why Sonnet 20 should appear at this point; nor is it clear whether the woman is addressing the lover or herself. Beauty is not to be bought:

> Beauty beyond all feathers that have flown
> Is free; you shall not hood her to your wrist,
> Nor sting her eyes, nor have her for your own
> In any fashion; beauty billed and kissed
> Is not your turtle; tread her like a dove—
> She loves you not; she never heard of love.

But what is this beauty? It would seem to be impersonal beauty, abstract and divine, the spirit of beauty in her lover. If so, the woman is cautioning herself. If not, and if the sonnet is a threat to the lover, the sonnet would correspond to earlier works of Millay in which the demands of beauty in art are exalted.

The next sonnet indicates a separation of the lovers—which proves unendurable to her. The affair is renewed with Sonnet 25. She is willing to disregard "wrath and scorn" as long as the experience is beautiful; and she is proud to be "heedless and wilful," like the "treacherous queens" of old who bore "Love like a burning city in the breast" (Sonnet 26). Sonnets 27 to and including 30 dwell on the raptures of love, too soon ended by dawn; the *carpe diem* theme appears in 28 and 29. Sonnets 29 to 32 assert more idealistically the lasting excellence of love in the face of destroying time. Sonnet 33 is premonitory of grief and loss: "Desolate dreams pursue me out of sleep;/Weeping I wake; waking, I weep, I weep." Then in Sonnet 34 the lover is chidden for voicing doubts which are likely to cause the death of their love; very fervently she begs, "Believe that I shall love you till I die;/Believe. . . ." This reaction is the beginning of the end, for she too has doubts of his constancy (Sonnet 35); she finds him wavering (Sonnet 36), envisions their love-city destroyed (Sonnet 37), and quotes his excuses for ending their love (Sonnet 38), to which she replies: "Oh, tortured voice, be still!/Spare me your premise: leave me when you will." The decisive break comes in Sonnet 39, where her pride and bitterness flash out: "Love me no more, now let the god depart,/If love be grown so bitter to your tongue!"

Yet she still has a generous spirit, and though in the remaining sonnets there are ups and downs of feeling—for the pangs of re-adjustment are severe before she achieves resignation—she refuses to disparage him; she insists on sincerity, for she is too proud to compromise or temporize. Sonnet 52 implies a parallel between this devastating love affair and that of Endymion and Diana.

Many readers felt that in *Fatal Interview*, as in earlier work, Millay was striking a distinctly modern note.[15] She stressed the mortality of the lover by representing him as an aggregation of chemicals (Sonnet 1). The woman of the sonnets is married, it seems, although she mentions her husband only in Sonnet 2:

> Unscathed, however, from a claw so deep
> Though I should love again I shall not go:
> Along my body, waking while I sleep,
> Sharp to the kiss, cold to the hand as snow,
> The scar of this encounter like a sword
> Will lie between me and my troubled lord.

Sophisticated enough to anticipate an end to her love-sickness, she is also a modern love-partner in her scorn for conventional coquetry and shrewd "love tactics"; her feelings are simple, direct, unconcealed:

> But being like my mother the brown earth
> Fervent and full of gifts and free from guile,
> Liefer would I you loved me for my worth,
> Though you should love me but a little while,
> Than for a philtre any doll can brew,—
> Though thus I bound you as I long to do.[16]

With her modern philosophy of love she disapproves of possessive-ness, yet finds herself driven by the old need to possess: instinct conflicts with her sense of honor. An indepedent creature, proudly high-minded, this woman exposes herself inevitably, it would seem, to injury and disappointment.

Along with the candid and realistic expression of passion, one finds in a small number of the sonnets a realism of detail that again shows the poet's awareness of nature—flowers and birds, storms and seasons—and country people's responses to it. The suggestion of the frost-ruined garden in Sonnet 35—"These pale and oozy stalks, these hanging leaves/Nerveless and darkened, dripping in the sun"—is beautifully accurate. Here, as in others of this kind, exact observations become impressive through a triumph of meticulous diction. Reviewers who could not commend the whole sequence found Sonnet 36 best; in it was a personal memory vividly presented, realistic and completely convincing:

> Hearing your words, and not a word among them
> Tuned to my liking, on a salty day
> When inland woods were pushed by winds that flung them
> Hissing to leeward like a ton of spray,
> I thought how off Matinicus the tide
> Came pounding in, came running through the Gut,
> While from the Rock the warning whistle cried,
> And children whimpered, and the doors blew shut;
> There in the autumn when the men go forth,
> With slapping skirts the island women stand
> In gardens stripped and scattered, peering north,
> With dahlia tubers dripping from the hand:
> The wind of their endurance, driving south,
> Flattened your words against your speaking mouth.[17]

There are similar details in sonnets 38, 42, and 43, although in the two latter, the description seems carried on too long. Sonnet 46, while it is less detailed, is another example of fine diction transmitting country experience.

Whatever reservations critics felt regarding the content or the total success of *Fatal Interview*, they accorded Millay high praise for her exquisite craftsmanship. Reviewers chose most often to quote Sonnet 11—followed by 30, 36, and 52. In my opinion the finest sonnets are 3, 7, 11, 30, 36, and 46. Almost as excellent are 2, 6, 31, 39, 45, and 52. High in technique are 5, 12, 24, and 33. The sonnets are Shakespearean in rhyme-scheme, but in about half of them Millay incorporated the final couplet into a sestet which becomes a firm unit like the sestet of a Petrarchan sonnet. Notable examples of such sestets are in sonnets 2 and 3 (already quoted), 5, 11, 39, and 46. The sestets of 2 and 3 are excellent for their rhythm, as are sonnets 6, 11, 39; and 7, 35, and 36 are among those with the unincorporated final couplet. "The effortless perfection of form, the opulence of language, the felicity and variety of the music, the poise of the accent, the crescendo and diminuendo within each sonnet, the unmistakable legato which marks the control of the great artist—all these are . . . evident. . . ."[18] The caesura is very successfully managed in the sestet of Sonnet 2 and in sonnets 7 and 11. Sonnet 11 is a single sentence with its parts most skillfully disposed, especially in the sestet:

> Love in the open hand, no thing but that,
> Ungemmed, unhidden, wishing not to hurt,
> As one should bring you cowslips in a·hat
> Swung from the hand, or apples in her skirt,
> I bring you, calling out as children do:
> "Look what I have!—and these are all for you."

Since *love* is the object of the second *bring*, after the parentheses of lines 9-10 the flow of the verse moves triumphantly to reach a crest with *I bring you* in line 13, followed by the falling cadence of the rest of the line, the crescendo of the first two feet of line 14, and then the quiet close. How effectively the simple country details of the sestet contrast with the artificiality of the casket, lovers'-knot, and ring of the octave.[19]

Alliteration and assonance are magnificently used in many of the sonnets, and the couplet of Sonnet 7—"No one but Night, with tears on her dark face,/Watches beside me in this windy place"— illustrates her capacity for legato and ritardando. Sonnet 7 contrasts acutely with Sonnet 6, in which the lines throb with increasingly rapid tempo to match the impatience of the speaker.

Millay was not exploring any new philosophical territory in this sequence. The sonnets are those of the Feminist, hedonist, and rebel of earlier volumes—praising beauty, defying Time, glorifying intense fulfillment while brief life lasts, and also interpreting the emotional vicissitudes of a woman in love. They do so, however, with greater poignancy and perhaps more universal appeal than in earlier poems.

IV   Wine from These Grapes

Wine from These Grapes shows Millay's poetry becoming increasingly objective and philosophical. Although the volume contains a few personal, reflective lyrics, it has no personal love poems. The character of the book is determined mainly by the sequence of eighteen sonnets, "Epitaph for the Race of Man"; the relation of mankind to nature, the relation of the individual to society, and the qualities of mankind are the themes not only of the sonnets but also of many of the other lyrics. According to Edmund Wilson, Millay was working in 1920 on a long poem in iambic tetrameter entitled "Epitaph for the Race of Man."[20] In 1928 ten sonnets under that title were published in the St. Louis *Post-Dispatch*, and later Millay added other sonnets to the series. Typescripts in the Ficke Collection at the Yale Library show that she made various alterations and grappled with problems of organization before publishing the sequence in a book.[21]

Sonnets 1-5 constitute a first section, prophesying Man's disappearance and making one see the whole range of earth-history from a far past to a distant future. Sonnets 6-11 show constant activities of Man throughout his history and illustrate his heroic capacities. Sonnets 12-13 are on his alienation from the rest of nature; and the last section, sonnets 14-18, emphasizes his tendencies to self-destruction which will cause the human species to become extinct.

Sonnet 1 is prophetic of a time when the stars will be off their courses and earth will be destroyed by collision with Vega, the great star in the constellation of the Lyre. By that time, however, Man will "be no longer here." Sonnet 2 focuses on the dinosaur, a species which vanished ages ago—"the veined and fertile eggs are long since cold." Sonnet 3 is addressed to the "cretaceous bird," evolutionary successor to dinosaurs at the time when toothed birds died out and both birds and mammals appeared, man among them—man in embryo as early mammal "out of ooze/But lately crawled, and climbing up the shore." According to Sonnet 4, earth simply cannot distinguish Man from other expressions of nature; it has no way to give special place or value to Man's uniqueness. Yet Man had great knowledge and powers of expression, even the power, ironically enough, to foresee his own extinction (Sonnet 5). After he is gone, no other tongue in nature will have the ability to tell of his exploits.

Sonnet 6 is one of the most impressive poems of the sequence. It emphasizes the everlasting stars; "Capella with her golden kids" has not changed since the day of the pyramid-builders, the Egyptian rulers who piously followed their religion because "their will was not to die." The sonnet ends with deft ironical understatement: "And so they had their way; or nearly so." The next four sonnets show Man's courage and endurance portrayed in his struggle at an early stage of civilization in the tropics against other animals for mere survival and in his energy and determination in the face of destruction wrought by earthquake, volcano, and flood. Always he looked to the future:

> . . . I saw him when the sun had set
> In water, leaning on his single oar
> Above his garden faintly glimmering yet . . .
> There bulked the plough, here washed the updrifted weeds . . .
> And scull across his roof and make for shore,
> With twisted face and pocket full of seeds. (Sonnet 10)

In fact, Sonnet 11 suggests that disasters had advantages; they brought out kind feelings, they produced co-operation—"for then it was, his neighbour was his friend."

Sonnet 12 depicts the parallel occupations of farmer and ant—both go out to milk; both must endure the conditions of earth. But they remain separate. Man ignores or perhaps disowns his kinship with other creatures. Nowhere in the rest of creation, according to Sonnet 13 (which seems to parallel Robinson Jeffers' ideas), is there such a disturbing, alien element as Man. "Earthward the trouble lies": though capable of knowledge, as of astronomy, he is narrow and intolerant—". . . and unamazed/Goes forth to plough, flinging a ribald stone/At all endeavor alien to his own."

Sonnet 14, a kind of summary of the previous section, is another tribute to Man's qualities; but it prophesies that fratricidal struggle will cause his extinction. In Sonnet 15, on the same theme, "the questioning mind of Man" explores the universe and fears the eventual annihilation of earth; but Man need not fear this, for he will annihilate himself earlier "in intimate conflict." Man bears a "bad cell," Sonnet 16 conveys, an element of "wild disorder"

> . . . destined to invade
> With angry hordes the true and proper part,
> Till Reason joggles in the headsman's cart,
> And Mania spits from every balustrade.

This figure, though developed as a picture of revolution, is ultimately Platonic: reason, which ought to rule in the harmonious personality, is overthrown by will and appetite. In fact, Greed is

Man's betrayer. Sonnet 17 explains Man's self-destruction with an elaborate metaphor: "Only the diamond and the diamond's dust/ Can render up the diamond unto man. . . ." And Man, able to survive all outward assaults, similarly destroys himself, "being split along the vein by his own kind." The last sonnet in the series envisages Man "cut down to spring no more, . . . even in his infancy cut down. . . ." And by what power?—"Whence, whence the broadside? whose the heavy blade? . . ./Strive not to speak, poor scattered mouth; I know."

Millay evidently did not intend the sequence to be regarded as a gloomy, dispiriting pronouncement. She told Grace King in 1941 that "Epitaph for the Race of Man" was her "challenge" to men to thrust out the "bad cell" and that she was expressing "her heartfelt tribute to the magnificence of man."[22] "Epitaph for the Race of Man" exemplifies Wordsworth's statement that "poetry is the breath and finer spirit of all knowledge; it is the impassioned expression which is in the countenance of all science."[23]

Critics have paid more attention to the panoramic breadth of imagination these sonnets exhibit than to their technique, which is generally excellent. Millay set herself difficult patterns; she followed the Petrarchan form in all except sonnets 1 and 6, which have Shakespearean octaves. Sonnets 13-15 open with emphatic inversions, and thus with a more formal tone than most, but all the sonnets are dignified. Occasional personifications, as in Sonnet 16, seem old-fashioned. Sonnet 18 begins with lines appropriately filled with continuants—*l, s, m, n, r*—"Here lies, and none to mourn him but the sea,/That falls incessant on the empty shore,/Most various Man. . . ." Alliteration and assonance are used with great skill in both 17 and 18.

Of the several poems allied to "Epitaph for the Race of Man" the finest is "The Return." It also emphasizes the failure of human society, which depletes and defiles Man, the simple animal son of earth. Nature, mindless source of countless men and other species, cares nothing for the success or failure of any species; she can give no special regard to Man,

> Who has no aim but to forget,
>   Be left in peace, be lying thus
> For days, for years, for centuries yet,
>   Unshaven and anonymous;

> Who, marked for failure, dulled by grief,
> Has traded in his wife and friend
> For this warm ledge, this alder leaf:
> Comfort that does not comprehend. (*CP*, 271-72)

Judging by history, Man cannot meet the demands of society, even the domestic circle or friendship; it is better then, and preferable, that he revert to the unself-conscious animal life. But earth-comfort is the comfort of death to man as it is to any other animal.

The poet's disillusionment during the early 1930's[24] shows in "Apostrophe to Man (*on reflecting that the world is ready to go to war again*)," which is a vehement satirical snort. In "My Spirit, Sore from Marching," she also reveals her loss of hope for human betterment, advising her spirit, ". . . sore from marching/ Toward that receding west/Where Pity shall be governor,/With Wisdom for his guest," (*CP*, 303) to "cleave henceforth to Beauty;/Expect no more of Man." By Beauty she means, one takes it, the cold impersonal beauty of Nature—indifferent Nature.

The difficulty of removal from human society comes out, however, in several poems, most personally in "Desolation Dreamed Of" and more effectively in "On the Wide Heath" and in "How Naked, How without a Wall." Probably "On the Wide Heath" (*CP*, 300-1) has an English setting because England is so settled a land, as stanza two suggests. The quatrain pattern, pentameter alternating with trimeter, is unusual;[25] and the rhythmic effects are extremely good. The whole poem is one long sentence in which "home," the initial word in four lines, is emphasized—a "home" as disagreeable as possible but tolerated—"it being/Too lonely, to be free," as Millay finally interprets the situation. "How Naked . . ." (*CP*, 311-12) stresses more the pain of trying to travel independently. With such phrases as "whispering ditch," "rising chill," "tiny foot," and "helpless shadow," the poem expresses vividly, on both the literal and the symbolic level, the nervousness and fears of the night-farer and the deadliness of his exposure "when other men are snug within" their comfortable, orthodox opinions.[26]

The personal lyrics of *Wine from These Grapes* also show more objective consideration of the poet and her relation to a world in which she has to accept age and death. "The Leaf and the Tree" (*CP*, 298-99) deals with the problem of the individual and the species: "When will you learn, my self, to be/A dying leaf on a living tree?" Presumably the individual should acquiesce in his situation, feeling that he has lived for a higher good, the good of the race, the improvement of mankind: "Has not this trunk a deed to do/Unguessed by small and tremulous you?/Shall not these branches in the end/To wisdom and the truth ascend?" Yet no tree lives forever; the species too will disappear in time. The individual's foreknowledge of death is a premonition of this fact: "The fluttering thoughts a leaf can think,/That hears the wind and waits its turn,/Have taught it all a tree can learn."[27]

The group of six poems beginning with "Valentine" was written in memory of Mrs. Millay. Each has its own form. The tetrameter couplets of "Valentine" have a seventeenth-century air. "Childhood Is the Kingdom Where Nobody Dies" is a free-verse piece presenting homely details of American life. "The Solid Sprite Who Stands Alone," a poem in the Housman manner, stresses the same "crooked me," the incorrigibly emotional woman, who appears in other lyrics. "Spring in the Garden" is in quatrains with lines of irregular length; and "Time, that renews the tissues of this frame" is one of the poet's best Petrarchan sonnets. The finest poem in the group is "In the Grave No Flower." A poem in harmony with others, like "Moriturus," it emphasizes the omnipresence of weeds on earth—dock, tare, beggar-ticks, thistles, and many more—"but there no flower." The choked voice of grief is perfectly rendered with abrupt, short, stabbing lines:

> . . . here
> Dandelions,—and the wind
> Will blow them everywhere.
>
> Save there.
> There
> No flower. (*CP*, 285)

Wine from These Grapes deserved the approval it received from various critics on the grounds of maturity, development, and a tautening of line comparable to the change from earlier to later Yeats.[28]

V *Flowers of Evil*

Millay's preface to *Flowers of Evil* supplies important information for the assessment of the Dillon-Millay translations of

Baudelaire. She assumes, first, that the shape of a poem is very significant; and, consequently, she approves of Dillon's decision to translate each poem in the same meter and form that Baudelaire had used. Thus the majority of the poems in the collection have been translated into hexameters instead of into pentameters, the staple of English poetry. The decision that a poem in translation should have not only the meaning of the original but also the same look and something of the same sound accounts for the fact that the translators had to elaborate many of Baudelaire's lines, just as Baudelaire himself, translating the eight-syllable lines of Longfellow's *Hiawatha* into alexandrines, was forced to elaborate.[29] Allen Tate remarked that "since French words are longer than English words," one who decides to translate into hexameters "is likely to put into the English a good deal that was not in the French."[30]

Translations, like grammars, are always imperfect; and, on the basis of their principles, considerable freedom must be conceded Millay and Dillon. Millay acknowledged that they found they got closer to their desired effect by introducing one or two extra syllables into a hexameter line, that they were bitterly aware of necessary losses in translation, that some of the poems were very freely rendered, and that translation often entails differences in terms of concrete detail and generality.[31] In fact, Millay anticipated most of the objections raised by reviewers of the book.

The Millay-Dillon *Flowers of Evil* contains seventy-two poems, nearly half of Baudelaire's published poetry. Thirty-six were translated by Millay, thirty-five by Dillon, and one, "The Fleece" (*La Chevelure*), by both. "The Fleece," like many of the others, illustrates the unevenness of the translations when they are judged in terms of precision and economy. Stanzas one and three are not very accurate: the figure is altered in line 6: *Je la veux agiter dans l'air comme une mouchoir!* becomes "I long to rake it in my fingers, tress by tress!" And lines 11-12 introduce extra abstract terms: *J'irai là-bas òu l'arbre et l'homme, pleins de sève,/Se pâment longuement sous l'ardeur des climats*: becomes "There where the sap of life mounts hot in man and tree,/And lush desire untamed swoons in the torrid zone." But stanzas 2, 4, and 5 are well done and parts of stanzas 6 and 7, though "glittering with

many a star" (line 31) and "every stone that gleams" (line 37)
are commonplaces that dilute the poetry; "sycamored" of line 38
seems brought in only for the rhyme.

"The Portrait" too reveals some of the inevitable shortcomings
of Millay's translations:

> *Qui, comme moi, meurt dans la solitude*
>
> . . . .
>
> *Noir assassin de la Vie et de l'art,*
> *Tu ne tueras jamais dans ma mémoire*
> *Celle qui fut mon plaisir et ma gloire!*

becomes

> Which, like myself, in dusty solitude
> Subsides. . . .
> O black and rude
> Assassin of proud Life and powerful Art:
> You cannot rob my memory of one thing,—
> Her, that was all my triumph, all my heart. (47)

The addition of the adjectives (*dusty, proud, powerful*) and the
use of *subsides* for *meurt* and of *rob* for *tueras* weakens the effect
of the poem. Also *heart* and *triumph* only obliquely suggest *plaisir*
and *gloire*.

Millay translated several of Baudelaire's most substantial
poems: *Rêve Parisien, L'Invitation au Voyage, Les Litanies de
Satan, Les Sept Vieillards, Une Martyre, Le Voyage, and Bénédiction.* Her rendering of *Bénédiction* has extra phrases: line 1,
"On a certain day"; line 4, "in scorn"; line 12, "reeking of stale
lust." Yet much of the poem is good—for example, stanza 6:

> *Pourtant, sous la tutelle invisible d'un Ange,*
> *L'Enfant déshérité s'enivre de soleil,*
> *Et dans tout ce qu'il boit et dans tout ce qu'il mange*
> *Retrouve l'ambroisie et le nectar vermeil,*

which Millay translates:

> Meantime, above the child an unseen angel beats
> His wings, and the poor waif runs laughing in the sun;
> And everything he drinks and everything he eats
> Are nectar and ambrosia to this hapless one. (261)

Line 3 is precise; and of the rest one can complain only that "runs laughing" scarcely does justice to *s'enivre* and that the vivid *vermeil* is omitted.

"Travel" (*Le Voyage*) is rather wordy, yet often suggests the quality of the original. The next-to-last stanza, however, with the famous address to *Mort, vieux capitaine* is unsatisfactory: *O Mort, vieux capitaine, il est temps! levons l'ancre!/Ce pays nous ennuie, ô Mort! Appareillons!* becomes "Oh, Death, old captain, hoist the anchor! Come, cast off!/We've seen this country, Death! We're sick of it! Let's go!" (245). Even allowing utmost freedom to the translator, one must boggle at this rendering as too undignified, too modern.[32]

"Invitation to the Voyage" makes an advantage of short curling and sweeping run-on lines (Millay's run-on lines are sometimes a drawback in the rendering of Baudelaire's hexameters). The refrain, "There, restraint and order bless/Luxury and voluptuousness," is a fairly good substitute for *Là, tout n'est qu'ordre et beauté,/Luxe, calme et volupté.* In general, the stanzas are well rendered although the last half of stanza 3 loses something of Baudelaire's effect because of a different order of details and the weakly general "all things in sight" (77).

Millay does best with the poems of Baudelaire which express sordid qualities of Parisian life, to which he was especially sensitive, and the *spleen* they induced. Her translation of *Une Martyre* ("Murdered Woman") is very good, particularly the last stanza:

> In vain your lover roves the world; the thought of you
> Troubles each chamber where he lies:
> Even as you are true to him, he will be true
> To you, no doubt, until he dies. (207)

The end of "Parisian Dream" is handled very well (57-59), and "Dawn" (*Le Crépuscule du Matin*) conveys accurately the seedy, dismal, O-God-not-again impression of *le sombre Paris* (169-71). Some of the sonnets are excellently done also, such as *Spleen I, Brumes et Pluies* ("Mists and Rains"), and *La Cloche Fêlée* ("The Cracked Bell").

Millay the ironist was a congenial translator of *L'Imprévu* ("The Unforeseen"); in it, as in *Bien Loin d'Ici* ("Ever So Far From Here"), she produces very well the tone of cutting ironical disgust, the sarcastic rebuke of Baudelaire's rasped, fastidious exasperation. The theme of hastening Time, which obsessed Baudelaire, was also congenial to Millay; her translation of *L'Horloge* ("The Clock") is one of her best.

In spite of the praises of Paul Valéry, Llewelyn Powys, and Lucie Delarue-Mardrus that were printed on the dust-jacket of *Flowers of Evil*, the reviewers had reservations about it, although all praised it in part. Whitridge, perhaps the most sympathetic of them, felt that Millay and Dillon had "sometimes sacrificed the rigor" of Baudelaire's thought; he believed that their Baudelaire was "altogether too easy-going."[33] If many of Millay's translations have in them more of Millay than of Baudelaire, the reader should not be surprised. Nevertheless, many of them are more accurate than other translations of Baudelaire.

CHAPTER 7

'The Sorrows of the Savage World'

I   Conversation at Midnight

MILLAY counselled readers to consider *Conversation at Midnight* in terms of a play rather than of a narrative poem (Foreword, viii). It is not, however, a play in the usual sense; it is a dialogue among seven men of differing backgrounds and beliefs who meet for an evening of conversation and drinking—literally, for a symposium. From its Platonic beginnings the dialogue form has had a great history. It flourished during the Renaissance, being used for discussions of all kinds of subjects: love, ethics, religious debates, witchcraft, and dramatic poesy. Though used less in modern literature, the form is still not dead.

John Peale Bishop said that Millay's characters are only "dramatized points-of-view" and that her work would lack the staying power of a dialogue like *The Courtier* in which the characters were real, being Castiglione's friends.[1] Granted that *Conversation* shows only a modicum of characterization, one might better place it with the "philosophical" novels of Peacock, such as *Headlong Hall*, than with either *The Courtier* or a stiff set-piece like Dickinson's *A Modern Symposium*, as Wilson suggested.[2] Millay's work, like Peacock's, allows people representing current ideologies to explain themselves and attack their companions' crotchets.[3]

Something of Millay's attitude during the time when she was writing *Conversation at Midnight* may be seen in the reports of an interview she gave on December 5, 1934, just after returning from two months of readings in the South. She told reporters she was disillusioned:

"I am disgusted with the hollow talk of disarmament. . . . We put wreaths on the grave of the Unknown Soldier, who's pretty damn well known by now as the symbol of the next war . . . while

Japan penetrates China. . . . We will never have peace so long as the interlocking munitions interests of Germany, France, England, control Governmental parties and influential groups . . . as long as people go on manufacturing death and trying to sell it. . . ."

"Do you think, then, that the profit system must be abolished?"

"Yes I blame the system . . . it goes back to the profit system . . . I should like to live in a world where everybody has a job, leisure for study, leisure to become wiser, more perceptive . . . I am willing to give up everything I possess, everything I ever will have . . . I am willing to live the simplest life . . . to live in a hut, on a loaf a day (Oh, I do know this sounds idiotic!) to achieve it. . . ."

"Do you want Communism?"

"No, no, I do not . . . Communism is repugnant to me . . . I am intensely an individualist . . . I cannot bear to have a thousand well-wishers breathe on my neck. . . ."[4]

Another report of the interview said that she "had hit on a compromise between the inequalities of capitalism and the universal rigors of communism." She did not explain herself in any detail, "but implied that her next book might have something to say about it."[5] The phrase "a thousand well-wishers breathe on my neck" shows that she was thinking of, if not writing, *Conversation at Midnight*. The expression appears, slightly altered, in the volume. In fact, the sonnet "Being out of love and out of mood with loving" had appeared in the *Saturday Evening Post* as early as December 6, 1930. Possibly *Conversation* had gradually been taking shape in her mind for several years.

From the start she planned to use a variety of metrical forms. The book is written, therefore, in a mixture of styles, comprising sonnets, some strict, others very free in meter; regularly structured lyrics; free verse; and verse with irregular line lengths and irregularly placed rhymes. The tone varies also: it is frequently colloquial, bantering, or satirical; only occasionally does it rise to dignity and eloquence. Though Millay thought well of *Conversation*, she considered the published version inferior to the one that was burned: "There were many passages which I had to re-invent, and others which I was forced to leave out entirely, so that the result is patchy and jerky."

The characters in the dialogue are chosen for diversity. The extremes of wealth and poverty, age and youth, are represented by

Merton, sixty-eight, a wealthy stockbroker, art-collector and lover of poetry, and by Lucas, twenty-five, an advertising writer who had to make a penniless start. The five other men are in their forties. Extremes of political commitment are represented by Merton, a Republican; Carl, a Communist poet; and Pygmalion, a cynic and hedonist disillusioned with politics. Extremes of religious belief are represented by Father Anselmo, a Roman Catholic priest, and Ricardo, an agnostic. John, a painter, has a religious nature but cannot thoroughly believe in anything. Ricardo, the host, is a liberal with a subtle mind. Though touching on many topics, their conversation focuses chiefly on the problem of religious, economic, and political faith. Millay divided the work into four parts, but the division has no significance.

As one first hears them, the men are talking about hunting and dogs, the sort of talk Millay heard at the home of George La-Branche, a neighbor in Austerlitz who was a wealthy stockbroker, pheasant raiser, and champion shot. Merton complains of paying five dollars a week for poor training and poor care of a dog. Carl's first comment is a sneer directed at the wasteful consumption of the wealthy. As one would expect of a Communist, Carl, a constant gadfly, is indignant over such waste; he feels the actuality of poverty and depression much more than the others, who are insulated by their wealth or their type of work. He believes that the depression-emergency must override any unproductive, pleasurable uses of leisure (8).

The conversation lights upon religious faith. Ricardo has suggested that John accept Faith "to frost with sugar the foul pill of Death" (9), but John finds it distasteful to take up with God "when you're an interested party" (11). Anselmo makes an analogy of the senses: probably a future age will lack the senses of smell and taste—and will it not then deny the possibility of there being five senses? The analogy leads to a discussion of human limitations, modern developments, and particularly airplane flight, which leads in turn to criticisms of the contemporary world—its noise and speed, the falsity and effectiveness of its advertising (from Lucas, who writes advertising copy), and its abuses of language. Anselmo regrets the degradation of Latin too, and the association with Church-Latin brings the talk back to the topic of Faith. This is a fair example of the method by which Millay conducts the dialogue; although she has it under control, the control is disguised by the spiraling progress of the talk often brought about through associations with subjects introduced by analogy or illustration. Thus the dialogue has a convincing realism.[6]

Ricardo expresses what seems to be a paradox: "It is I who have faith . . ." (26). For he believes in the existence of Mystery beyond his immediate horizon, and he accuses Anselmo of an arrogant anthropomorphism:

> You cannot conceive that there might be that of which
>   you cannot conceive; you are arrogant;
> You endow all things with human attributes; you do
>   not hesitate
> To call the inconceivable "Father." (27)

Anselmo gives a dignified defense of Faith arrived at by the light of Reason. Then the men discuss the questions: why do men fight? what chance is there for peace? John suggests that nations fight for elbow-room; Ricardo says that they fight for empire because man's largely animal nature includes a fighting instinct: Jesus' doctrine of brotherly love "is not characteristic of the species" (35). Anselmo thinks that there may be hope of development, wars being a kind of fermentation. Carl agrees but believes that this cannot happen under Capitalism: "Only in revolution, only in the audible seething of the crushed masses/Does Man ferment to a purpose, to his proper destiny (36). Ricardo and John see war as a betrayal of Man's best, as the means of debasement. Pygmalion, however, points out that "there's lots of men that love a fight" (38). War is so exciting that it won't be abandoned. Ricardo sadly philosophizes: "War is man's god; he has but one./And Peace, but the time it takes the unhorsed warriors to mount and come on" (39). Anselmo gives a priest's answer:

> There is no peace on earth today save the peace in the heart
> At home with God. From that sure habitation
> The heart looks forth upon the sorrows of the savage world
> And pities them, and ministers to them; but is not implicated.

He feels, however, that they cannot comprehend his attitude, and after playing some Bach on Ricardo's piano, he soon leaves.

With Part II, Lucas brings up the topic of love, particularly lost love. All the men join in criticisms of women, expressed in a witty parody of Ogden Nash's style; but the love-discussion mainly aids in characterization: one sees the youth and relative inexperience of Lucas (who has fewer than twenty speeches in the whole poem); the down-to-earth sensualism and cynicism of Pygmalion, already indicated by his remarks on war; and the deeper understanding of Ricardo, who is given two "arias"—"The family circumstance" and "If you lived in the north"—more sympathetic to the cause of women and idealistic love.

At times Millay records, as it were, remarks of only two or three of the talkers to each other and not to the company. So Merton explains to John the strength of economic motives, which reduce heroism in the modern world.[7] In the arguments that ensue, Carl and Merton chiefly oppose each other, although at times the rest are against Carl; but Ricardo occasionally defends his own position. When Merton and Ricardo attack proletarian poetry, Carl voices proletarian hopes, likening the dictatorship of the proletariat to a second coming. He identifies himself with workers and their dirt: "I honour the dirt . . ./Because it is the dress my mother wore" (66). He likens the Communists to a group of friends round a campfire which provides light; and, furthermore, he regards the dictatorship of the proletariat as inevitable—the triumph of Communism as simply the fulfillment of historical destiny, concerning which individual opinions or feelings can have no influence. Like a bomb falling from an airplane, it "can't be stopped" (69).

On the other side Merton complains against present-day vulgarity. He favors tradition, and Carl accuses him of simply not being able to accept change. Carl is, of course, an anti-traditionalist: the "Brocaded Past," he says, is a heavy "drag upon the shoulders" (71). Meanwhile, Ricardo regrets the modern Babel tower created by specialization: "this bean-stalk, Science" will not reach to God. "We have specialized ourselves out of any possible/ Acquaintance with the whole," and communication is no longer possible among men (71-72).

In Part III, the debate on the value of tradition continues, and Carl emphasizes present needs of "the living world!" (75). Merton and Pygmalion reveal themselves further as practical *hommes moyens sensuels* in their discussion of salmon fishing and horse breeding, among other matters; and Carl also shows that he is something more than a fanatic in his contribution to the discussion of mushrooms. Ricardo, the subtle-minded individualist, voices another "aria" on individualism and its difficulties ("The mind thrust out of doors," which recalls some of the lyrics in *Wine from These Grapes*) (78-79). He even argues for madness as the only means to freedom since "the intelligible has failed us on every hand" (85-86).

Carl and Merton clash again. Carl insists that there must be a revolution that will put machines to work for men. Ricardo points to the Communist record in Russia where Communism must be imposed by a dictator like Stalin, "the dissenting mouth stopped up with unarguable lead" (88). Merton sees in the Russian situation a dark prospect for culture; but Carl scoffs at conventional American "culture," which means going through gestures considered "correct" or merely collecting things "either old or rare" while sneering at anything beautiful but common. Carl expresses the best of the Communist aspiration in one of the finest lyrics of the volume:

> Beautiful as a dandelion blossom, golden in the green grass,
> This life can be.
> Common as a dandelion-blossom, beautiful in the clean grass
> Of the young, all-promising year;
> Beautiful to the child: the eye of the child is clear.
>
> Life itself is a weed by the roadside, a common, golden weed.
> Give us back the eyes of our childhood, freed
> From the squint of appraisal, the horny glint of greed!
>
> Beautiful as a dandelion-blossom, golden in the green grass,
> This life can be.
> Common as a dandelion-blossom, beautiful in the clean grass,
>   not beautiful
> Because common, beautiful because beautiful;
> Noble because common, because free. (90)

Seeing man as evil, Merton rejects, however, such ecstatic praise; he is disillusioned of any such hopes by the "recent altercations/ Within the Left"[8] (91). And both Ricardo and Pygmalion reprove Carl for emotionalism, for regarding Communism as religion when it is supposed to be science. In Part IV, Ricardo criticizes the lack of distinction under Communism; each person is only a cog in an impersonal machine. Merton accuses Communists of acting from base motives of hatred and not of love.

Midnight arrives. The company think of differing time-zones in Europe. Thus John has a chance to enforce the midnight-theme:

> . . . I fear that in Paris, too,
> It is midnight. Midnight in London; midnight in Madrid.
> The whole round world rolling in darkness, as if it
>   feared an air-raid.
> Not a mortal soul that can see his hand before his face. (97)

This metaphor of darkness—that of fear, ignorance, indecision—bitterly gives point to the title of the volume. Yet, Pygmalion surmises, Mussolini and Hitler see their way before them. Ricardo confesses to a bit of admiration for Hitler's Germany and even tells Lucas that he doubts if he would fight for things he cares most for: "I'm really in favour of having the human race wiped out" (98). This statement seems like an admission of extreme weakness and futility by the Liberal; but Millay may intend it as deep irony. In a moment Ricardo speaks vigorously in England's favor. When Carl challenges them to do something to prevent another war—to fight fascism instead of wringing their hands—they do not take up the challenge.

Carl pushes his attack further by accusing Merton (as a capitalist) of having failed and being unfit to rule. This is criticism after the Auden-Spender fashion. Merton retaliates with the charge that Communists enjoy freedom in a democracy which they deny in Russia. Carl's defense is lame; it amounts to assuming that criticism would be out of place under the perfect Soviet government. Carl is confident of Communist victory because of wholeness and undivided effort. Merton counters that these qualities also apply to Hitler, and Ricardo reminds them that "singleness of purpose and direct approach" belonged to many an extinct race "that knew what it wanted and followed its nose" (109). Carl applies the parallel to Capitalism—"a prehistoric monster."

Ricardo remains an arch-individualist; he believes in neither God nor Communism, and he dislikes the mass of people: "And I would rather stand with my back against an icy, unintelligible void/Than be steamed upon from behind by the honest breaths of many well-wishers" (111). His lot is particularly difficult. Carl taunts him with having no program. Ricardo admits the weakness of the liberal position—which is, in a way, its glory:

> Bright colour and insistent noise attract
> The multitude, without whose perilous favour
> We may exist, but cannot act.
>
> . . . .
>
> Only by self-defilement could a liberal party earn
> A place among the branded herds. . . . (112)

Even so, John finds hope in the liberal position—as an "insistent leaven" (113). Carl gloats over the coming victory of Communism; but Pygmalion roughly accuses Communism of not permitting independent thinking—Communism is the opium of the dissatisfied.

The hour grows late, and Ricardo's party grows louder and rougher. After they come at last to trading insults, Ricardo asserts himself as host and moderator to restrain his guests. They have another drink and soon leave—exhilarated and still friends. Nothing has been settled during the conversation. But during this dialogue the chief opposing political and social philosophies of the dark time of 1937 have been thrown into conflict. The assumptions of each speaker and the things he values most have been made clear. Each one has scored points against his opponents; Millay has kept the balance reasonably even, although her own sympathies are with Ricardo, the Humanist Liberal, the least opinionated and the most reasonable of the disputants.[9]

Few reviewers were enthusiastic about *Conversation at Midnight*. Some felt that Millay, not perceiving that the incendiary hand of Providence had been at work on Sanibel Island, had mistakenly dredged her memory and salvaged the work. It was too "modernistic," too prosy, too inconclusive. Perhaps, as Patton holds, reviewers generally did not see *Conversation* in the right perspective. It should be ranged, he believes, with the socially conscious, argumentative discussion plays of the 1930's written by Auden, Spender, MacNeice, and MacLeish.[10] Some of the same problems and attitudes appear in *The Dog Beneath the Skin* (1935) and *The Ascent of F 6* (1937) by Auden and Isherwood, MacNeice's satirical extravaganza *Out of the Picture*

(1937), and Spender's *Trial of a Judge* (1938). In general, however, these works are far more conventionally theatrical (though of expressionistic type) than *Conversation* is.

MacLeish's *Panic* (1935) has passages that are closer to the tone and spirit of Millay's work—for example, the denunciation of "the Revolution" by the financier McGafferty, which could as well be voiced by Merton or Pygmalion.[11] One may safely say that all these writers became socially conscious and felt that the socio-economic problems of the time demanded expression. Millay had earlier, in *Aria da Capo*, addressed herself to a dramatic problem in a special type of verse. She would have enjoyed expressing her penchant for satire, and obviously she became more and more concerned with the world situation. It was not uncharacteristic of her to write *Conversation*; and as a poetic technician, she must have liked working with the various meters she used.

In letters to the author, Witter Bynner praised *Conversation* as a symposium; and Maxwell Anderson its effectiveness as dialogue; he encouraged Millay to write actively for the theater.[12] In fact, given belated production in Los Angeles, November, 1961, *Conversation* played successfully for sixteen weeks;[13] and it was scheduled to go on tour, starting in October, 1964, prior to a New York engagement.

Though it has some lyric passages, *Conversation* comes mainly from the head and not the heart. Those who censure the work because it does not give a decisive message or because it is insufficiently lyrical are regarding it the wrong way. It may be censured, however, for too slack a prosiness at times—for example:

> Adult allegiance to an intellectually-conceived inevitable
>   proletarian dictatorship, does not exact,
> Necessarily, repudiation of a childhood memory, a
>   humiliating and meagre
> Personal experience, which as a matter of recorded fact
> Was largely instrumental in bringing about that stumbling
>   "approach". . . . (68)

Sudden shifts, too, from the loosely fingered lines to sonnets and "arias" take one unbelievably fast from one emotional level to another. Presently, the work may seem dated because of its topicality. It is, however, an interesting discussion; it is witty,[14] and, considering its colloquial quality, it is charged with a considerable amount of stimulating poetry.

II Huntsman, What Quarry?

Huntsman, What Quarry? came out in May, 1939, and represents work going back to 1934 and very likely earlier. Though it resembles earlier volumes, it has more poems on political-social matters; it contains, perhaps, more poetry of a philosophical cast, and less verse showing intense preoccupation with death. The volume opens with "The Ballad of Chaldon Down," a slight story with something of ballad manner and Chaucerian tone. The words of the ballad are put in the mouth of a sick man: "In April, when the yellow whin/Was out of doors, and I within,—". He would be Llewelyn Powys and is visited by a lady: "A lady came from over the sea,/All for to say good-day to me." The poem is a memorial of Millay's visit to Powys in the spring of 1934—

> All for to ask me only this—
> As she shook out her skirts to dry,
> And laughed, and looked me in the eye,
> And gave me two cold hands to kiss:
> That I be steadfast, that I lie
> And strengthen and forbear to die. (*CP*, 317)

The poem represents Millay's encouragement to Powys to recover from tuberculosis. It has a number of local references and catches very well the atmosphere of the Dorset coast.[15]

"The Princess Recalls Her One Adventure," restrained and effective, is an early-Millay-manner poem of disappointed love. The third stanza is especially good:

> We stood by the lake
> And we neither kissed nor spoke;
> We heard how the small waves
> Lurched and broke,
> And chuckled in the rock. (*CP*, 318)

"Modern Declaration"—a fiercely sincere statement, rather Whitmanesque, of steadfastness in love—is truly modern in its vocabulary and its honest recognition of circumstances likely to make a person compromise:

> . . . never through shyness in the houses of the rich or
>   in the presence of clergymen having denied these loves;
> Never when worked upon by cynics like chiropractors
>   having grunted or clicked a vertebra to the discredit
>   of these loves;
> Never when anxious to land a job having diminished them
>   by a conniving smile; . . .
>   declare
> That I shall love you always.
> No matter what party is in power;
> No matter what temporarily expedient combination of
>   allied interests wins the war;
> Shall love you always. (*CP*, 352)

The most impressive of the love poems is "Theme and Variations," a presentation of a woman involved in an affair with an unworthy man. She recognizes clearly his unworthiness; yet "rolled in the trough of thick desire," she suffers, saddened by the sordidness of the situation. Section IV is particularly Meredithian: the lovers scarcely bother to deceive one another; finally "even the bored, insulted heart" will "break its contract." Other loves made her proud, however difficult they were or inadequate she was; but this one hurts in a special way: "Not that this blow be dealt to *me*: /But by thick hands, and clumsily."

She can wish for the peace of the grave, but what she should do is to have enough strength of will to cut off the affair. At the end, however, she finds herself overly involved, perversely committed to this person who is not "fit subject for heroic song"; she cannot free herself: "That which has quelled me, lives with me, /Accomplice in catastrophe" (*CP*, 355-67).

"The Fitting" intimates the passion and seriousness of a love affair without saying anything directly about it. Probably the poem comes out of some time, perhaps 1932, when Millay was having dresses made in Paris. The poem depends on the contrast between the matter-of-fact ignorance of the fitter—"*Ah, que madame a maigri!*"—and the knowledge of the customer concerning the reason for her thinness, the seriousness of which she is not willing to admit even to herself. She makes an excuse to the fitter:

"C'est la chaleur." But, as the fitting goes on, her thoughts are with her lover, whose caresses she is contrasting with the handling she receives from the shopwomen:

> I stood for a long time so, looking out into the
>   afternoon, thinking of the evening and you . . .
> While they murmured busily in the distance, turning me,
>   touching my secret body, doing what they were paid
>   to do.[16] (*CP*, 342-43)

Implied is a contrast with the lover who does not have to be paid for his secret intimacies. Another poem, "Rendezvous," is about a calculated arrangement in Greenwich Village; in this affair a woman no longer young engages, taking pleasure from it, but no longer finding the pleasure of youth; for the poem ends with: "And I wish I did not feel like your mother" (*CP*, 341). But in contrast to these bitter-sweet poems is the joyous domesticity of "Thanksgiving Dinner," which celebrates the recovery from serious illness of "my love," who will receive "a banquet of beets and cabbages . . ." (*CP*, 330). The loss of more interesting food will be compensated for by this unromantic meal.

Among the sonnets "Be sure my coming was a sharp offense" and "Thou famished grave, I will not fill thee yet" are typical defiances of death. "Now let the mouth of wailing for a time" is an ironic challenge to mourners who believe in a Heaven and thus should not grieve: "Grief that is grief and worthy of that word/ Is ours alone from whom no hope can be/That the loved eyes look down and understand" (*CP*, 685). However she may have accepted Christian ethic and felt mystical reverence, Millay remained firmly agnostic.[17]

The defeat of democratic Spain, the appeasement of Germany and its expansion were incidents that drew Millay's interest. "Say That We Saw Spain Die" is a tribute to democratic Spain as a bull in a bull-ring dying brutally of loss of blood, no one daring to face it with sword. "From a Town in a State of Siege," a group of five sonnets not reprinted in later collections, is evidently based also on the Spanish War. When Bohemia-Moravia became a German protectorate on March 15, 1939, and Slovakia followed on March 16, Millay wrote the sonnet "Czecho-Slovakia," one of the best of her political poems.[18] Full of pity, she stresses the harshness of the time, the lack of honor and mercy. "The barking of a fox has bought us all" must refer to either Hitler or Neville Chamberlain. The betrayal-allusion at the end is a satirical triumph: "While Peter warms him in the servants' hall/The thorns are platted and the cock crows twice" (*CP*, 692).

"Lines Written in Recapitulation" and "This Dusky Faith," although confessions of failure to influence the course of the world, are vigorous assertions of a humanist faith in man. The other side of this coin is represented by the sonnets "Upon this age, that never speaks its mind" and "My earnestness, which might at first offend," the second much more successful than the first, which has a confused mixture of images, although it tries to be Wordsworthian.

The title poem of the volume is the finest among the philosophical pieces. The masculine and the feminine are contrasted—masculine dedication to action and violence, feminine conservatism and tenderness. One might think, with Rosenfeld, that the huntsman symbolizes man's endeavor to attain the Ideal or Truth or the Absolute, "the hot pads/That ever run before" (*CP*, 332). His ceaseless, demanding pursuit cannot be deflected by worldly pleasures.[19] The poem is pictorial, economical, and dramatic.

The sexual motif enters with "I, too, beneath your moon, almighty Sex," a defiant sonnet, in the old manner, that asserts that her work is absolutely sincere; it comes out of her far from perfect self and includes among various elements lust "and nights not spent alone" (*CP*, 688). "Menses" is far more original, a frank poetic representation of menstruation as a psychological problem in marriage. Its subtitle is: "He speaks, but to himself, being aware how it is with her," and it dramatizes the temporary nervousness, anger, impatience, and emotionality of women.

The finest of the personal poems is the autumnal, regretful but acquiescent "Not So Far as the Forest." With senses less keen, the middle-aged person begins to live in memory more than in the present, neglected because of familiarity:

> Night falls fast.
> Today is in the past.
>
> Blown from the dark hill hither to my door
> Three flakes, then four
> Arrive, then many more.

The approach of age is symbolized by a gradually dying tree; by the death of Love, unheroically stung by gnats in a swamp; and finally by the frustrated flight of a bird with clipped wing:

> Hopeless is your flight
> Towards the high branches. Here is your home,
> Between the barnyard strewn with grain and the forest tree.
> Though Time refeather the wing.
> Ankle slip the ring,
> The once-confined thing
> Is never again free. (*CP*, 335-39)

The poem expresses the poet's sense of loss—loss of keen response because of growing familiarity, acceptance of domesticity and things-as-they-are; loss of lyric capacity with the years. In essence this poem is her "Intimations Ode," in which she tells how the glory and the dream are gone. One may see, however, in much of the volume how years have brought the philosophic mind. The poems of *Huntsman, What Quarry?* come from a woman of forty who looks on life with some chagrin and who has learned to express herself at her best in language that is crisp, usually contemporary, and non-"literary."

III Make Bright the Arrows

Even before Millay wrote her bitter sonnet "Czecho-Slovakia" in March, 1939, she had perhaps written "Underground System" because she foresaw the alliance of Germany and Russia. On August 23, 1939, the German-Russian pact was signed; and World War II began with the German invasion of Poland on September 1. Though she had been ill, Millay decided on October 23 that she could appear at the *Herald-Tribune* Forum in New York the next day. There Millay criticized the atmosphere of neutrality; she favored repealing the Embargo Act of 1937 and hoped Americans would use their freedom of speech to assert pride in democracy and their sympathy with England and France. "As regards the war between a Germany whose political philosophy is repugnant to us, and an allied Britain and France whose concepts of civilized living are so closely akin to our own," why should Americans hesitate to say they hope Britain and France will win?[20] Thus Millay, consistently anti-fascist, favored a strong armed position for democratic nations; her common sense told her that pacifism or appeasement would be dangerous policies for the United States.

From the moment the Germans invaded the Low Countries on May 10, 1940, Millay began writing propaganda verse to stir American feeling for Britain and France, to attack isolationists, to dissipate the prevalent desire for neutrality and dread of involvement, and to create a feeling of pride and obligation toward democracy and of loathing for appeasers as well as oppressors. At the very moment when disaster fell on the British at Dunkerque "There Are No Islands, Any More" appeared in the *New York Times Magazine*, June 2, 1940—"Lines Written in Passion and in Deep Concern for England, France, and My Own Country." She might have included the Netherlands, her husband's country; for both felt concern about his relatives there; furthermore, the German conquest meant that Boissevain lost all his wealth abroad.

Millay's propaganda verse was collected in *Make Bright the Arrows; 1940 Notebook*, published late in November. The subtitle she hoped would indicate that the verse was unpolished; she spoke of the work as "posters" and as "acres of bad poetry." Evidently she hoped that by rousing the country to preparedness she would help to keep it out of war. In the title poem she says: "Stock well the quiver/With arrows bright:/The bowman feared/Need never fight" (vi). She explained her position in a long letter to her protesting friend, Mrs. Charlotte Babcock Sills, and spoke with feeling of sacrificing her carefully treasured poetic reputation for her country because many people would never forgive her for writing so poor a book.

Though critical readers honored her sincerity, they knew that the book at best was mere journalism—and, unfortunately, poor propaganda as well as inadequate poetry. Ficke thought it bad propaganda—"being so largely hysterical and vituperative . . . Its egocentricity repels the very people whom she wished to attract."[21] In too many places Millay fails to exhort and merely wields the lash. "Intelligence Test" and "Noël, Noël" are the most glaring examples.

The most acceptable pieces are "Memory of England" (written during the terrible bombings of England during October, 1940), in which she could dwell with vivid and loving memory on English experiences she and her mother had had; and some of the

sonnets. As a group, the sonnets fail to attain the exalted Wordsworthian patriotism and protest which is their goal. But "The Old
Men of Vichy," though not free of clichés, closes with concentrated scorn. The best sonnets are the two chosen for inclusion in
Collected Sonnets and *Collected Poems*, "I must not die of pity"
and "How innocent of me," the least hortatory in the volume.

IV   The Murder of Lidice

On June 10, 1942, the Nazi government announced that the
village of Lidice, Czechoslovakia (population 446), had been
razed; all the men killed; and the women and children sent to
labor camps. The Nazis committed this atrocity in reprisal for the
assassination of Reinhard Heydrich, the "protector" of Bohemia
and Moravia, who was known to the Czechs as Heydrich the
Hangman. Immediately the Writers' War Board requested Millay
to write a poem commemorating the destruction of Lidice.

The Murder of Lidice is a ballad set between introductory and
closing hortatory material. Life in Lidice is presented in terms of
the cycle of seasons, of work, of marriage: "First came Spring,
with planting and sowing;/Then came Summer, with haying and
hoeing;/Then came Heydrich the Hangman, the Hun . . ."(7).
Karel and Byeta grow up, become engaged, and are to marry on
June 10, 1942. The clairvoyant Byeta has premonitions that she
will never marry, and her father is fearful after he hears that
Heydrich has died and that the Germans are saying that people
in Lidice are hiding his killer. Byeta cries:

> "Mother, I run from room to room
> For I hear what nobody hears!
> Heydrich the Hangman howls in his tomb!
>
> ·   ·   ·   ·   ·   ·   ·   ·   ·
>
> He howls for a bucket of bubbly blood—
> It may be man's or it may be of woman,
> But it has to be hot and it must be human! (14-15)

Much is made of the horror of the executions, burnings, and
butchery on June 10. Karel crawls, dying, to Byeta; and she kills
herself rather than become the slave of a German officer. Millay
gives the situation the aspect of legend by reporting that people
say that on June 10 the village is still there, the citizens going

about their customary tasks. At the end she addresses "Careless America, crooning a tune:/. . . . Think a moment: are *we* immune?" (32).

The ballad style tends to mitigate the triteness of the writing; but except in parts dealing with the seasonal activities of the village, it is not a good poem. The style is reminiscent of nineteenth-century balladry, even of Poe's "Annabelle Lee" and Alfred Noyes' "The Highwayman." The clairvoyance of Byeta and the werewolf motif applied to Heydrich seem mere conventional props. Like most of Millay's propaganda verse, *The Murder of Lidice* is overdone; instead of rising, it falls from emotional strain.

More interesting than such material written to assignment are the poems Millay wrote to indicate the spirit in which she thought the war must be waged and the world reconstructed later. The idealistic "Not to Be Spattered by His Blood," written soon after Pearl Harbor was attacked, expresses her confidence in American victory (". . . for I shall surely kill him; he is numbered already with the dead") and her concern that ethical values might be utterly destroyed in the war. Should the warrior be stained by the dragon's blood of hate and "bring infection to city and town," it would be better to let the enemy beast live. Millay told Grace King that "we must conquer the forces in our own hearts that breed hatred and enmity among men."[22]

"To the Leaders of the Allied Nations," published in January, 1945, shows Millay's old radical distrust of Establishments and a democratic desire for a radically renovated world. She demands that the leaders exhibit blueprints for "a new/World—a decent one this time, a world a man might live in without shame." She says there are hints of chicanery and of welching on their promises; and she speaks in the name of " 'Common Men' " for a world where "men and nations, shall be free." Evidently she hoped that the results would be better than those of World War I, for she says Americans "at this war's end/Not only hope, but, yes, by God, intend/To see our dreams come true!"

V Mine the Harvest *and* Collected Poems

The posthumous volume *Mine the Harvest* is an epitome of Millay's poetry, but it shows a greater reflective cast. Here, as often before, are poems on the intensity of her experience, which she finds almost unbearable. In "This/Is mine, and I can hold it" (*CP*, 448) she tells of her ecstasy listening to a thrush singing: ". . . I may be shattered/Like a vessel too thin/For certain vibrations." And in "The sea at sunset can reflect" she describes the beauty of the sea, the stars, and the Northern Lights—the last experience, paradoxically, an ordeal. These poems are not far in spirit from "God's World," but the verse has greater intellectual control. "How did I bear it . . ." (*CP*, 530) contrasts the intense sense impressions of childhood with her response to the loveliness she encounters as a mature woman ". . . grown up and encased/ In the armour of custom"—even prudently wearing rubbers. The experience is still almost overwhelming.

The first two sonnets of the collection also represent a looking back on intense experience—in "Those hours when happy hours were my estate,—" as on the gardens of an estate now "looked at through an iron gate." It cannot be revisited, but "I smell the flower, though vacuum-still the air;/I feel its texture, though the gate is fast" (*CP*, 719). In the following sonnet Millay insists that for her, reality has been as splendid as her dreams; her experiences of "music, and painting, poetry, love, and grief" have been almost unbearably intense (*CP*, 720).

One of her ecstasies, too, had been reading. How real the world of fiction was to her as a child she brings out in "To whom the house of Montagu."[23] This sweetly whimsical piece is in tetrameter, largely in run-on couplets, and contains but one sentence, fifty-one lines long. She smiles at herself as a girl, thinking how close and intimate and indiscriminately mingled in her imagination were the people and settings of *Romeo and Juliet*, *Don Quixote*, The Troy story, *Venus and Adonis*, *Hero and Leander*, and the world of classical mythology. In her world ". . . naked long Leander swam/The Thames, the Avon and the Cam," and "any man in any wood"

> . . . could ride
> A horse he never need bestride—
> For such a child, that distant time
> Was close as apple-trees to climb,
> And apples crashed among the trees
> Half Baldwin, half Hesperides. (*CP*, 447)

Millay was not primarily a nature poet, but the feel of life intensely experienced in various places comes through convincingly. "The American scenes she knows are set down with a truth unsurpassed in American poetry," wrote Cook.[24] In *Mine the Harvest* her accustomed vividness of observation suffered no lessening. "The Strawberry Shrub" (*CP*, 455) is perhaps the finest example of her use of the meticulously, exquisitely exact detail. References to the senses and to "colour of the key of F" may relate the poem to *Conversation at Midnight*. The description of the flower in terms of Greece is startlingly apt—"Not graceful, not at all Grecian, something from the provinces:/A chunky, ruddy, beautiful Boeotian thing." The quaint, old-fashioned flower jibes with the name of Dorcas, the girl who is to show it at school.

Another brilliant descriptive poem is "New England Spring, 1942." In places it is the spirit of the season that is conveyed; in others, precise images, as of the tapping of maples, the birds about the pails, and the return of snow. The rush of long lines and the check and wheel of short ones are well handled. The close relates the poem to the theme of unendurable beauty: "And Spring is kind./Should she come running headlong in a wind-whipped acre/Of daffodil skirts down the mountain into this dark valley we would go blind" (*CP*, 470).

A somewhat similar piece of exact description is "Look how the bittersweet . . . ," which deals with autumn. The poem indicates with a special sense of immediacy in its third stanza how the might of nature in a short while easily overcomes the works of man, such as the pridefully erected stone wall broken and "bought up by Beauty now" (*CP*, 543). The description of the northern jay in "Sky-coloured bird . . ." is so detailed that it seems labored although every point is exact. Whereas much of her late work is sharp and spare, one may hear in this poem, as occasionally elsewhere, an unusual richness of sound through internal rhymes.

Since the poet suffered the importunities of visitors at Steepletop (cf. *Cave Canem, CP*, 499-500; and "What chores these churls do put upon the great," *CP*, 727), no wonder she appreciated the Nirvana-like tranquillity and purity of her island, as she tells of it in the partially descriptive "Ragged Island." In this poem there are excellent samples of that "fascinating tension of timing" which Millay achieved in much of her latest poetry.[25]

Mine the Harvest has few poems on love and death. The sonnet "Admetus, from my marrow's core I do/Despise you (*CP*, 726) is the dramatic monologue of a proud feminist Alcestis satisfied to die not because of love for Admetus but out of bitter disillusionment because her love for an unloving husband has died. Millay returned to the story of Sappho in "Of what importance, O my lovely girls" (*CP*, 451). The speaker is a Sappho who thinks poetry is no longer honored in "a world so loud." Therefore, she is going to take her life—although the disappearance of her poetry would be her real death.

Mine the Harvest contains some poems of a kind not seen before in the poet's work—poems apparently based on dreams. The first of these is the mysterious "Dream of Saba." It recounts, beginning in a sort of journalistic style, the coming of a hurricane upon a ship in the Leeward Islands, of which Saba is a part. The danger of shipwreck is vividly described, and then the miraculous lifting of the ship by a "wave like a giant's palm" into the crater of an extinct volcano, where the ship remained. The poem concludes with "The sky above our bowl is blue" (*CP*, 486). "Dream of Saba" may possibly have religious significance, but it seems not to have the right context for a religious poem.

"When the tree-sparrows . . ." begins with a beautiful description of sparrows in apple trees at dawn—birds that made the poet forget a dream she had been having which involved danger to a loved person. She wept, "yet clawed with desperate nails at the sliding dream . . ." but continued to weep—". . . frozen mourning melted by sly sleep,/Slapping hard-bought repose with quick successive blows/until it whimper and outright weep" (*CP*, 489). This poem may have been written after her husband's death. A final section opens abruptly, telling of the tides, and counselling against tears: "Oh, do not weep these tears salter than the flung spray!—/Weepers are the sea's brides . . ./I mean this the drowning way." In "Some Things Are Dark" Nightmare speaks, emphasizing its blackness, compared to which nothing else can seem dark.

Such poems may reflect the poet's interest in her psychological states during years of nervous strain and ill health. "Intense and terrible, I think, must be the loneliness" deals with a more general psychological condition: the fearful clinging of babies to some loved object that provides security after unwelcome departure from the womb. A baby resents ". . . the crimson betrayal of his birth into a yellow glare./The pictures painted on the inner eye-lids of infants/just before they sleep/Are not in pastel" (*CP*, 549). The poem ends forcefully because of the contrast with pastel nursery colors stressed earlier.

Among the personal poems of *Mine the Harvest* are several sonnets. "Now sits the autumn cricket in the grass" associates the changing of happiness into grief for someone "who died on Michaelmas" with the changing of summer into autumn. After the mention of things that have disappeared with autumn—aconite, roses, swallows, phlox, and asters—the last line, "Nor can my laughter anywhere be found" (*CP*, 733), comes as the perfect summation of one of Millay's finest Petrarchan sonnets. Millay had told Elizabeth Breuer in 1931: "I am a very concentrated person as an artist. I can't take anything lightly. . . . the nervous intensity attendant on writing poetry . . . exhausts me, and I suffer constantly from a headache."[26] Her headache is the subject of "And must I then, indeed, Pain, live with you," a stoical-sardonic sonnet in which the poet sees Pain as a parasitical partner in her whole life; at least it is an evidence of being alive, though it has harmed her. Understatement is usual in these sonnets, as in the final couplet: "You will die with me: but I shall, at best,/Forgive you with restraint, for deeds like these" (*CP*, 734).

She reflected too upon the grief with which she was acquainted during her last years. In the sonnet "Felicity of Grief!—even Death being kind," the challenge of grief is like a glove, once light and easy to ignore; but to the suffering one it becomes weighty. Thus grief brings felicity in the thought that it could not be so heavy if the loss had not been so great: "Think—of how great a thing were you bereft/That it should weigh so now!—and you knew/Always, its awkward contours, and its heft" (*CP*, 737). Both this poem and the rather involved sonnet "Grief that is grief and properly so hight" lack line seven in the octave.

The chiseled lyric "The courage that my mother had" (*CP*, 459) is a fine tribute to New England strength of character; the free-verse piece "At least, my dear" (*CP*, 436) tells something of her thoughts regarding her husband after his death. She is like a shepherd trying to collect her thoughts like sheep; they are "cropping the mind-bane," memories of deeds that caused him pain. At least he was spared the pain of seeing her die and living thereafter: "The most I ever did for you was to outlive you./But that is much."

The sonnet "If I die solvent—die, that is to say," suggests a reason for continuing to bear the pains of life—the obligations of her poetic power. Life is a "dark wood," the *selva oscura* of Dante, in which, assailed by wolves (of pain and illness?), she fears that for survival she may have to throw them everything she values. If not, " 'Twill be that in my honoured hands I bear/ . . . . An earthen grail, a humble vessel filled/To its low brim with water from that brink/Where Shakespeare, Keats and Chaucer learned to drink" (*CP*, 735).

In two sonnets she comments on her writing of propaganda verse: "To hold secure the province of Pure Art" and "And if I die, because that part of me" (*CP*, 723-24). They represent her considered opinion[27] that she did well to write her impure verse trying to defend what she believed in. Though rather Wordsworthian, they are stiff and self-conscious. More interesting is "I will put Chaos into fourteen lines" (*CP*, 728), Millay's comment on the process of creating poetry. It is based on the folk-motif of the shape-changer. Chaos is to be held "in the strict confines/Of this sweet Order," the order of the sonnet. The sestet speaks of the hours and the years of the poet's struggle against Chaos, finally victorious. "Something simple not yet understood" is a telling phrase for the amorphous material of a poem which the poet at last shapes and controls.

Musings and decisions about the human condition are presented in numerous poems of *Mine the Harvest*. One of the most noteworthy is the long "This should be simple." If one had God-like power, it should be simple—starting fresh and creating from nothing—to bring into being a world "at least as beautiful and brave/ And terrified and sorrowful as ours" (*CP*, 461). How much greater an achievement would be the creating, now, of good out of accumulated evil—the evil that pervades every part of men's lives. Millay states, regretfully, that man has never rightly come to flower, and she indignantly points out many human deficiencies. Efficient persons, accepting evil, can manipulate this world; those devoted to the ideal are hurt and baffled: "Evil alone has oil for every wheel" (*CP*, 465). In spite of disappointments and difficulties, however, she still retains some hope that the world will be improved: we are not up to the task, but future generations may accomplish it: ". . . in some way, yet, we may contrive/To build our world; if not this year, next year" (*CP*, 467). Her romanticism does not include the conviction that man or the world is naturally good; it is, rather, in a vision of future improvement that her romanticism consists.

At times man's evil obscures the vision, as in the sonnet "Read history: so learn your place in Time" (*CP*, 730). She regards history as a repetitious cycle of wars; and, in the twentieth century, warfare has simply been extended through invention and made more efficient. The cycle will continue until men at last root out war. A similar distrust of modern cleverness and intellect appears in "We have gone too far" (*CP*, 427).

"The Animal Ball" (*CP*, 430) satirically stresses the difficulty of man's surmounting his animal inheritance. He tries to disguise himself as a human being, but "The reek of the leopard and the stink of the inky cat/Striped handsomely with white, are in the concert hall. . . ." The sonnet "Read history: thus learn how small a space" (*CP*, 731) places man among hunting beasts in a world of struggle and death where he must protect his little space. Man deserves a special tribute, however; for he is the only animal that knows he must die. And, in the face of that knowledge, he accomplishes everything he does—things to be marveled at: "But what a shining animal is man,/Who knows, when pain subsides, that is not that,/For worse than that must follow—yet can write/Music; can laugh; play tennis; even plan." Once more Millay's admiration for human capacities comes out, as it did in "Epitaph for the Race of Man."

In an even finer sonnet, "Tranquility at length, when autumn comes," Millay symbolizes the coming of old age through the arrival of autumn. Summer was a time of action: "to broaden, raise,/proceed, proclaim, establish"; but autumn will allow the mind to be free "One moment, to compute, refute, amass,/Catalogue, question, contemplate, and see . . ." (*CP*, 721).

For the human condition freedom and courage are the essentials. "Not for a Nation" is Millay's great affirmation of freedom. Can man as a species survive? Will not lizards, sharks, and cutworms outlive him? Here is the theme again of "Epitaph for the Race of Man"—man who has weakened himself by division and nationalistic suspicions, hatreds, and wars. Millay rejects loyalty to divisive principles like nationalism:

> Not for a nation,
>
> . . . .
>
> Not for the flag
> Of any land because myself was born there
> Will I give up my life.
> But I will love that land where man is free,
> And that will I defend.
> "To the end?" you ask, "To the end?"—Naturally, to the end.
>
> (*CP*, 553-54)

She shows how dearly she appreciates the life of America, familiar and secure; but she treasures most the ideal of human freedom held up by the founders of the United States. One might consider the poem an extension of "To the Liberty Bell." Those "Periwigged men/Sitting about a table" who maintained the dream of freedom may have been

> . . . men with more vision, more wisdom, more purpose,
>   more brains
> Than we,
> (Possibly, possibly)
> Men with more courage, men more unselfish, more intent
> Than we, upon their dreams, upon their dream of Freedom,—
>   Freedom not alone
> For oneself, but for all, wherever the word is known. . . .
>
> (*CP*, 557)

Here is another challenge—it comes out in the reiterated "Possibly, possibly"—to the greatness of man and, specifically, of Americans. Here, Millay has the last word in her long lovers' quarrel with America.

The poet sometimes used Christian symbols to convey man's sense of sin and need for repentance and hope (cf. "Christmas Canticle," *CP*, 425-26), but her religious attitudes were those of an agnostic concerning the immortality of the soul—according to Grace King, her "mature opinion concerning the Ultimate."[28] In "The Agnostic" Millay describes the situation of an agnostic with very effective images: first, faith is a clearing in a forest—". . . a clearing sunned so bright/He cups his eyeballs from its light" (*CP*, 492); then it is the white light that he can never see, although he is aware of all the colors of the spectrum—"But light evades him: still he stands/With rainbows streaming through his hands." With all his uncertainties, the agnostic is reverent. His attitude is that of John in *Conversation at Midnight*; he would not be a hypocrite and betray his "own heart, which bids him, 'Praise!'" Millay felt, like Tennyson, that "There lives more faith in honest doubt,/Believe me, than in half the creeds." But, like many agnostics, Millay honored the Christian ethic and the imperishable influence of Jesus, as may be seen in "Jesus to His Disciples" (*CP*, 502). Perhaps Humanistic Stoicism might describe Millay's attitude best. A Stoic temper is implied in many of her poems, especially those in which she speaks of enduring pain and loss.

Mine the Harvest and *Collected Poems* close with a sonnet once part of "Epitaph for the Race of Man"—"What rider spurs him from the darkening east." She projected her imagination into the past as well as the future. The "little bell without a tongue" is flung by the horseman who shouts "Greetings from Nineveh!"; and it reminds man of his ties with the past and his likeness to ancient kingdoms long gone down. The implications of the sonnet were as clear to the poet in the 1920's as when she died five years after the bombing of Hiroshima.

The twenty sonnets of *Mine the Harvest* (only three in the Shakespearean mode) are nearly as good as any that Millay ever wrote. They are packed and rather more intellectualized than most earlier ones, and on that account seem somewhat angular. Whether in long rippling lines or in tetrameters, her poetry in this posthumous volume is controlled and simple, not artificial nor contrived. It conveys the flavor of living in a world of wonders past or present, the endurance of griefs amid the world's evils. One is impressed by its thoughtful quality: the whole volume has a "sober coloring" that comes from maturity and the intensely serious regard the poet cast upon life in her later years.

CHAPTER 8

'The Thumbers of the Record'

CRITICISM of Millay's work has swung from almost unani-
mous praise during her early career to extreme neglect and
disparagement since her death. For the first dozen years following
the publication of *Renascence and Other Poems*—all through the
1920's—Millay was in high favor. Only *A Few Figs from Thistles*
received much critical disapproval.[1] She was regarded as a leading American lyric poet and was thought particularly representative of the younger women of the day with their determination to
be free of old, shackling conventions. In 1927 Edward Davison
placed her next to Frost and Robinson in America, praising her
fervor and control while deprecating her tendencies to fever and
exaggeration. He was rather troubled by her outspokenness although he thought it possible that ultimately her breaking through
traditional reticence would be considered a virtue.[2] Among her
works "Renascence," *Aria da Capo*, and many sonnets, especially
"Euclid alone," received the most consistent approval.

With the appearance of the Sacco-Vanzetti poems in *The Buck
in the Snow*, readers began to wonder whether Millay was de-
cisively turning to poetry less subjective, more philosophical and
filled with social consciousness. Some critics thought these poems
might be portents of a new Millay.[3] Her next volume, *Fatal Interview*, however, showed her still subjective and still preoccupied
with the theme of love. The year of its publication, 1931, saw
numerous appraisals of her work, some of which stressed its traditional quality. McInnis thought she did well not to try to meet
public demands for novelty in expression.[4] So did Lewisohn, who
in 1932 praised the elemental and timeless in her poetry: she had
"not been put to the sterile shifts of mere innovation and experiment. . . ."[5]

Allen Tate's review of *Fatal Interview* perhaps gave the most perceptive appraisal. Tate noted that Millay had received both adulation from admirers and patronage from those suspicious of her popular success. He found her a distinguished poet of the second order, primarily a writer of sensibility who used the vocabulary of nineteenth-century poetry to convey twentieth-century emotion; she brought that language back to life by employing it as her personal idiom: "she has been from the beginning the one poet of our time who has successfully stood athwart two ages. . . ."[6]

As the 1930's continued, Millay received less praise. Some thought her work repetitious; her vocabulary was said to be "literary" or "bookish"; the question was raised whether she could become "mature." The vogue for the intellectualist poetry of Donne on the one hand and the liking for oblique expression and surrealistic cloudiness on the other combined to make her directness seem old-fashioned. As early as 1935 Edmund Wilson commented on the cycle of praise-disparagement that Millay had been put through—as had numerous other contemporaries.[7] *Conversation at Midnight* was widely regarded as a mistake; it was too unlyrical and too different from Millay's usual mode to produce much satisfaction. For all the general sympathy with her aims, the propaganda writings of 1939-41 dismayed many readers; and after the publication of *Collected Sonnets* (1941) and *Collected Lyrics* (1943), critics lost interest in Millay.

Her death caused a number of appraisals to be published in 1950-51, the most sympathetic that of Rolfe Humphries, who attacked the prevailing attitude of depreciation. He thought her a fine lyric poet who could "write so memorably that her language was on every tongue" and who, in spite of occasional failures and shortcomings of taste and feeling, had wit and "clarity, mastery of epithet, control of modulation." In her later work "the lyric quality persisted, graver, more reflective, a little sorrowful for being wiser, a good deal subtler as the rhythms were moved to the more pensive mood."[8]

Criticism since her death has tended to find her work so tinged with the spirit of the 1920's that it is dated. Yet her work has not lacked for readers. Publishing records and the experience of Norma Millay at Steepletop show that many people discover, and many continue to read, her work with enthusiasm. Readers find many things in her work to be enthusiastic about. In an age of criticism and poetical dryness, the lyrical intensity of personal revelation in her poetry is striking. Her work is romantic and for the most part subjective. Though Millay, like other poets, puts on more than one *persona*, the reader always perceives the woman who identifies herself by her compassion, her love of beauty, her idealism, her tough unwillingness to compromise, her vehement defense of what she considers right.

Millay told Elizabeth Breuer that readers liked her poetry because she wrote of things that most people had experienced, such as "love . . . [,] death, and nature, and the sea. Then, too, my images are homely, right out of the earth. . . . I have an age-old simplicity in the figures I employ."[9] This elemental quality—her fierce clinging to life, her unabashed treatment of love, her constant awareness of death—reveals also a definable personality contending with the world and doubly insures a wide appeal for her work.

The bookishness of her poetry has been exaggerated. She was a well-read woman and had a wide range of vocabulary. Often, and especially in dramatic monologues, she wrote in colloquial style. Often, and especially in sonnets, she wrote in a formal style. It is a mistake to imply, as some critics have done, that the hallmark of her poetry is a kind of would-be grand manner that is faded and artificial. There are times when she is pompous and others when she indulges herself in girlish coyness. She has a tendency to use easy personifications which suggest centuries earlier than the twentieth; but for the most part, and increasingly through her whole career, her diction and style are not conspicuously "literary," old-fashioned, or derivative. Although she was at her mature best in elegiac poems, reflective sonnets and poems of exact description, Millay covered a considerable range in her work. In addition to her ambitious sonnet sequences, "Renascence," *Aria da Capo*, and *The King's Henchman* stand out as peaks of her success.

Rarely is her personality absent. Whether in poems with physical setting or in more abstract works, her sincere revelation of a modern woman is exact and strong. As a woman writer she is in the tradition of Lizette Woodworth Reese, Anna Hempstead

Branch, and Sara Teasdale; but she surpasses all of them in power and boldness. Millay's feminism served her well in breaking down the conventionalities that they largely observed. Millay was responsible for destroying the restrictions upon women's expression and the prejudices against women's frankness. Women even yet are not so thoroughly emancipated, however, that her feminism is dated. In addition, her feminine sensitivity both to beauty and to moral issues is one of the values of her work.

Without technical excellence these attitudes and ideas would mean nothing, of course, as poetry. In technique she bridges the time of Tennyson and the twentieth century. According to W. Adolphe Roberts, Tennyson and Housman were her acknowledged masters.[10] The Tennysonian and early Pre-Raphaelite attention to detail and sonority she adopted naturally. For use of the exact word and for subtle matchings of sound and sense her best work bears comparison with that of the finest masters of English poetic technique. In the line of poets who stress predication,[11] she often uses long sentences with numerous qualifiers. Such sentences help to give a formal air to much of her poetry.

In her sonnets she soon reached a high level of achievement which she maintained throughout her career. Her example did much to restore the sonnet to respectability during her time.[12] She deserves credit for success in the Petrarchan sonnet, which she wrote more and more with advancing years. She occasionally admits syntactical looseness and metaphorical inconsistency to her sonnets; but at her best, as Humphries indicated, she brought to the sonnet "much of the virtue of Latin elegy—the clarity, the point, the balance of sound, the limitation of sense—which she has studied with so much profit and so much affection."[13]

Although she is largely tied to tradition through her sonnets, her writing after 1928 is not bound to the traditional iambus and trochee or to traditional stanzas; she chooses her forms freely, sensitively exploring the possibilities of varied rhythms and lines of varied length. So sophisticated a reader as Winfield Townley Scott thought her work contained "a surprising number of ventures into free verse. . . ."[14] Neither a hard-shelled traditionalist nor a fanatical experimenter, Millay followed an eclectic course.

Millay's constant theme is devotion to freedom. The freedom of the individual, the freedom of woman completely to be an individual—these values engage her complete loyalty. The ideals of freedom and justice, paramount among the traditional values of America, lead her to denounce threats to these ideals. As a supporter of freedom and justice she is a loyal citizen and a loyal critic of her country, although indignation unfortunately betrays her into shrillness. She became at times a prophetess-poet, never hesitating to speak her mind on public matters—thoroughly American in the tradition of Emerson, Whitman, Whittier, Lowell, and Moody. Yet, while possessing "a large sense of America," as Francis Hackett pointed out, she also had a reverence for life that extended "beyond all sentient individual beings and so to universal being. . . ."[15] Every creature that endures the pains and ecstasies of earthly life is awarded the dignity of compassionate regard.

Hers is a radical creed. Meaningful freedom includes the freedom of the human being to be himself, to retain his integrity and fearlessly to express his individuality. Without belief in conventional religion Millay becomes a radical humanist, a Humanist-Stoic. Divisive modern forces, atomistic in their effects, have impelled many twentieth-century people along the same course. They find in Millay a poet who provides a moving record of a full-bodied participant in the twentieth century and who enunciates a credo for private lives and for public issues.

Notes and References

If the source is recorded in the Bibliography, the note is listed only by author and page. When more than one work by an author has been cited, the works have been identified. Material from Letters of Edna St. Vincent Millay has not been noted.

Chapter One

1. Shafter, p. 29.
2. Gurko, p. 9.
3. *Ibid.*, pp. 24-26.
4. Shafter, p. 59.
5. Gurko, p. 18.
6. The sonnet was printed for the first time (along with commentary) in the Foreword to *Collected Sonnets of Edna St. Vincent Millay* (1941).
7. Gurko, p. 34.
8. Patton, pp. 35-37.
9. Gorham Munson, " 'More Sea than Land Am I': Edna St. Vincent Millay and the Town of Camden," in *Penobscot: Down East Paradise* (Philadelphia, 1959), p. 172.
10. William Wordsworth, Preface to *Lyrical Ballads*.
11. Munson, p. 234.
12. *Flowers of Evil*, Preface, p. xxiii.
13. Letter of Ferdinand Earle to Arthur Davison Ficke, December 3, 1912, in the Arthur Davison Ficke Collection in the Yale University Library.
14. *Ibid.*
15. Orrick Johns, *Time of Our Lives* (New York, 1937), p. 204; Jessie B. Rittenhouse, *My House of Life* (Boston, 1934), pp. 250-51.
16. Carpenter, p. 166.
17. Rittenhouse, p. 252.
18. Gurko, p. 50. That such an occasion provided the genesis of "Recuerdo" is also supported by Floyd Dell, Norma Millay, and W. Adolphe Roberts.
19. E. H. Haight, "Vincent at Vassar," *Vassar Alumnae Magazine*, XXXVI (May, 1951), 14.
20. *The Hickory Limb* (New York, 1950), p. 25.
21. Her roles were as follows: Sylvette in Rostand's *Les Romanesques*, February 27, 1915; Marchbanks in Shaw's *Candida*, March 5, 1915; Marie de France in *The Pageant of Athena*, October 11, 1915; Deirdre in Synge's *Deirdre of the Sorrows*, March 11, 1916; Vigdis in

Notes and References

Masefield's *The Locked Chest*, December 9, 1916; a part in Lagerlöf's *The Christmas Guest*; the Princess in her own *The Princess Marries the Page*, May 12, 1917.

22. *The Hickory Limb*, p. 91.

23. Agnes Rogers, *Vassar Women. An Informal Study* (Poughkeepsie, New York, 1940), p. 67.

24. *The Hickory Limb*, pp. 25-26, 92.

25. Max Eastman, *The Enjoyment of Living* (New York, 1948), p. 298.

26. *The Hickory Limb*, pp. 211-12.

27. *The Fiftieth Anniversary of the Opening of Vassar College. October 10 to 13, 1915. A Record* (Poughkeepsie, New York, 1916), p. 234.

28. *The Hickory Limb*, p. 212.

29. Dorothy A. Plum and George B. Dowell, comps., *The Magnificent Enterprise: A Chronicle of Vassar College* (Poughkeepsie, New York, 1961), p. 48.

30. Carpenter, p. 232.

Chapter Two

1. Floyd Dell, *Homecoming: An Autobiography* (New York, 1933), p. 299.

2. Gurko, p. 89.

3. Information given me by Norma Millay, July 4, 1964.

4. Malcolm Cowley, *Exile's Return* (New York, 1934), pp. 57-58.

5. Dell, *Homecoming*, p. 246.

6. Frederick J. Hoffman, *The Twenties* (New York, 1955), p. 35.

7. Cowley, p. 59.

8. Information in private letters to me.

9. Helen Deutsch and Stella Hanau, *The Provincetown, A Story of the Theatre* (New York, 1931), pp. 7, 20.

10. Sheldon Cheney, *The Art Theatre*, rev. ed. (New York, 1925), p. 68.

11. *A Victorian in the Modern World* (New York, 1939), p. 314.

12. *Homecoming*, p. 304.

13. Cowley, pp. 69-71.

14. *Homecoming*, p. 301.

15. *Selected Poems* (New York, 1926), p. 182.

16. Dell, *Homecoming*, p. 307; Gurko, pp. 98-100.

17. According to a Ficke letter at Steepletop, he sailed February 19, 1918.

18. The sonnet was published in *Reedy's Mirror* and in Houston Peterson's *The Book of Sonnet Sequences* (New York, 1929) but not collected later.

19. In line 4 the poet replaced *fire* with *flame* and *white* with *sharp*.

20. *Selected Poems*, p. 64.

21. W. Adolphe Roberts, "Tiger Lily" (unpublished memoir of Millay in the Vassar College Library), p. 3.

22. *Ibid.*, pp. 2-7, 9-10, 17-18.

23. "My Friend Edna St. Vincent Millay," *Mark Twain Journal*, XII (Spring, 1964), 2.

24. *Homecoming*, p. 315.

25. King, p. 166.

26. *Homecoming*, p. 304.

27. Gurko, pp. 93-97.

28. *The Improper Bohemians* (New York, 1959), p. 265.

29. Breuer, pp. 50-52.

30. Langner, *The Magic Curtain* (New York, 1951), p. 120.

31. *The Theatre Guild: The First Ten Years* (New York, 1929), p. 35.

32. *The Magic Curtain*, p. 97; Helburn, *A Wayward Quest* (Boston, 1960), p. 55.

33. King, p. 100.

34. "There Are War Plays and War Plays," *New York Times*, December 14, 1919, Sec. 8, p. 2.

35. Wilson, *The Shores of Light*, p. 751.

36. Rittenhouse, *My House of Life*, pp. 253-55.

37. *The Shores of Light*, pp. 764-66.

38. Though Wilson says she was disillusioned on this score, "having tried two Greenwich Village ménages" (*The Shores of Light*, p. 766), Floyd Dell states (in a private letter) that since Millay lived with her sister and later with her mother and sister in the Village, she never lived with a man in a household that could be called a ménage. Very likely, however, Wilson is right concerning her opinions.

39. Evidently Kennerley found himself on occasion in financial difficulty. Vachel Lindsay complained in 1914 that Kennerley owed him some $400 and would not answer letters. Carpenter, *Sara Teasdale*, p. 189.

40. Hoffman, *The Twenties*, pp. 336-37, 355, 379.

41. Cowley, pp. 223-24.

42. Wilson, *The Shores of Light*, p. 754.

43. Frank Crowninshield, "Crowninshield in the Cubs' Den," *Vogue*, CIV (November 1, 1944), 158.

44. Wilson, *The Shores of Light*, pp. 767, 769.

45. Gurko, p. 146.

46. *The Shores of Light*, p. 766.

47. Alfred Kreymborg, *Troubadour* (New York, 1925), p. 376;

48. Letters in the Yale Library.
49. Grace Hegger Lewis, *With Love from Gracie* (New York, 1955), p. 197.
50. A copy of the dummy of *Hardigut* is in the Yale Library.
51. *With Love from Gracie*, p. 187.
52. Information given me by Charles Ellis, July 4, 1964.
53. Harold Stark, *People You Know* (New York, c. 1924), p. 280.

Chapter Three

1. Information in a letter from Floyd Dell, June 25, 1963. The poems added were "Recuerdo," "Macdougal Street," "Midnight Oil," and "To Kathleen."
2. These were numbered as follows in *The Harp-Weaver and Other Poems*: 1, 12, 4, 9, 19, 22, 8, 11.
3. Joseph Freeman, *An American Testament* (New York, 1936), pp. 246-47.
4. *Homecoming*, p. 398.
5. Max Eastman, *The Enjoyment of Living* (New York, 1948), p. 521; *New York Times*, August 31, 1949; New York *Herald Tribune*, August 31, 1949; *Homecoming*, p. 309; *The Shores of Light*, p. 771; Allan Ross Macdougall, "Husband of a Genius," *Delineator*, CXXV (October, 1934), 41.
6. *Homecoming*, p. 398.
7. A copy of the contract is in the Arthur Davison Ficke Collection in the Yale University Library.
8. Ficke wrote this in January, 1924. Manuscript in the Arthur Davison Ficke Collection.
9. *Equal Rights*, November 24, 1923, p. 327.
10. Hoffman, *The Twenties*, p. 335.
11. In the Arthur Davison Ficke Collection in the Yale University Library there is a telegram of this date from Millay to Ficke.
12. *An Institute of Modern Literature at Bowdoin College, Brunswick, Maine* (Lewiston, Maine, 1926), pp. 58-63.
13. *Commemorative Tributes of the American Academy of Arts and Letters, 1942-1951*. "Edna St. Vincent Millay" by Deems Taylor, p. 107.
14. *New Yorker*, III (February 19, 1927), 18.
15. Information from Mrs. Arthur Davison Ficke in a letter of July 7, 1963. A copy of the poem in the Arthur Davison Ficke Collection is entitled "For Gladys and Eugen, entreating them to take good care of Arthur" and is inscribed "with love, Jan 8, 1927 *Vincent*."
16. Patton, pp. 156-57; Gurko, pp. 175-77.
17. *The Survey*, LVII (November 15, 1926), 205; Gurko, p. 181.

18. *New York Times*, May 5, 1927, p. 12; May 6, 1927, p. 25; May 7, 1927, p. 4.

19. *Ibid.*, July 28, 1927, p. 1; August 4, 1927, p. 1.

20. *Ibid.*, August 5, 1927, pp. 1, 4, 5; August 6, 1927, p. 2; August 7, 1927, pp. 1, 23; August 8, 1927, p. 2.

21. *Ibid.*, August 9, 1927, pp. 1, 3-4; August 10, 1927, pp. 1-2; August 11, 1927, pp. 1, 3; Jeannette Marks, *Thirteen Days* (New York, 1929), pp. 1-2, 8, 9-10; Michael A. Musmanno, *After Twelve Years* (New York, 1939), p. 303.

22. *New York Times*, August 21, 1927, Sec. 1, p. 18.

23. First published in *The Liberator*, October, 1922; reprinted in *May Days; an anthology of Verse from Masses-Liberator*, ed. Genevieve Taggard (New York, 1925), p. 187.

24. *New York Times*, August 22, 1927, pp. 1-2; Musmanno, pp. 341-43; Marks, p. 26.

25. *New York Times*, August 23, 1927, p. 4; Marks, pp. 28-30; Musmanno, pp. 387-88; Arthur Garfield Hays, *Let Freedom Ring*, rev. ed. (New York, 1927), pp. 337-38.

26. *New York Times*, August 24, 1927, p. 2; *Letters of Edna St. Vincent Millay*, pp. 223-24.

27. *Ibid.*, August 25, 1927, p. 10; Yost, pp. 62-65.

28. William Miller, *A New History of the United States* (New York, 1958), pp. 350-56.

29. King, pp. 5, 6, 132, 138-39.

30. Jerome Beatty, "Best Sellers in Verse: the Story of Edna St. Vincent Millay," *American Magazine*, CXIII (January, 1932), 103.

31. Macdougall, "Husband of a Genius," *Delineator*, CXXV (October, 1934), 40-41.

32. Beatty, pp. 102-4.

33. *The Shores of Light*, pp. 790-91.

34. Cablegram in the Yale University Library.

35. *New York Times*, December 17, 1928, pp. 23, 27.

36. Information from George Dillon in a letter of April 24, 1964.

37. For illustrations of Millay's remarkable memory see Gurko, p. 56, and Carl J. Weber, "A Poet's Memory," *Colby Library Quarterly*, Ser. IV (1958), 265-72.

38. King, p. 143.

39. *Ibid.*, p. 203.

40. On November 5, 1940, the day of the election, Millay issued a statement urging voters to thwart the plot against the third-term tradition. New York *Herald Tribune*, November 5, 1940, p. 27.

41. Max Eastman intimates that excessive drinking played a part in the falling-off of Millay's writing: "There is no doubt that chemical stimulation blunted the edge of Edna's otherwise so carefully cherished

genius." *Great Companions*, p. 103. On the other hand, drinking may have softened the intolerably sharp edges of these difficult years so that they could be borne.

42. *The Shores of Light*, p. 787; *Great Companions*, pp. 101-2; Harrison Dowd in an interview of June 14, 1964.

43. Letter in the New York Public Library.

44. Letters of September 23 and 28, 1949, from Margaret Cuthbert to Mrs. Ficke, in the Arthur Davison Ficke Collection in the Yale University Library.

Chapter Four

1. *The New Era in American Poetry* (New York, 1919), p. 272.

2. "First Books of Verse," *Poetry*, XIII (December, 1918), 167.

3. Donald Smalley, "Millay's 'Renascence' and Browning's 'Easter Day,'" *Bulletin of the Maine Library Association*, III (February, 1942), 10-12.

4. Untermeyer, *American Poetry Since 1900* (New York, 1923), p. 214; Dell, *The Literary Spotlight*, p. 86; Davison, pp. 675-76.

5. Witter Bynner, "Edna St. Vincent Millay," *New Republic*, XLI (December 10, 1924), 14.

6. *The New Era in American Poetry*, p. 274.

7. Petitt, p. 123. Edmund Wilson thinks that the storm in "Renascence" also stands for sexual love. *The Shores of Light*, p. 759.

8. Seventy-two out of 171 published sonnets are Petrarchan; and there are others with the Petrarchan sestet.

9. King, p. 82.

10. Cf. Seneca, *Hippolytus*, 1. 607: *Curae leves loquuntur, ingentes stupent* (Light troubles speak; great ones are dumb).

11. Van Doren, p. 110.

12. *The Literary Spotlight*, p. 81.

13. Llewellyn Jones, *First Impressions* (New York, 1925), p. 113.

14. Carl Van Doren compared her poems to Suckling's. *Many Minds*, p. 111.

15. Pp. 105-7.

16. In Yost, p. 19.

17. *The Shores of Light*, p. 768.

18. O. W. Firkins, "'Second April' (An October View)," *Independent*, CVII (November 19, 1921), 194.

19. Colum, p. 189.

20. *The Shores of Light*, p. 759.

21. In Yost, p. 23.

22. *New Republic*, XLI, p. 14.

23. *The Measure*, No. 7, September, 1921, p. 17.

24. Colum, p. 189.

25. Kreymborg, *Our Singing Strength*, p. 442.
26. Walter Gierasch relates the imagery of the poem to Ecclesiastes. *Explicator*, II (May, 1944), 23.
27. This line (*Inferno*, V, 113) comes from Dante's pitying comment after he has heard the first part of Francesca's explanation of her love affair with Paolo: "What sweet thoughts, what desire led these lovers into this painful pass." After his comment Francesca tells how she and Paolo were reading the book of Lancelot mentioned at the end of Millay's sonnet.
28. Colum, p. 189.
29. See note 18 above.

Chapter Five

1. Preface to *The Princess Marries the Page*, p. xi.
2. *Ibid.*, p. xii.
3. The play has a few touches reminiscent of the style of Beulah Marie Dix. See Patton, pp. 70-71.
4. Patton, p. 47.
5. Haight, "Vincent at Vassar."
6. Cf. Millay's production notes in the Walter Baker edition, pp. 39-48. A typescript of these notes is in the Vassar College Library.
7. King, p. 100.
8. Information from Floyd Dell in a letter of June 25, 1963.
9. *Behind a Watteau Picture* (Boston, 1918), p. 62.
10. She had a part in *Jack's House*. Kreymborg, *Troubadour*, pp. 314-16.
11. *New York Times*, December 14, 1919, Sec. 8, p. 2.
12. Harriet Monroe, *Poetry*, XXIV (August, 1924), 264; XXX (April, 1927), 46; Van Doren, p. 110; Kreymborg, *Our Singing Strength*, p. 445; Brenner, p. 74; Dell, *Homecoming*, p. 267; Atkins, p. 77; Cargill, p. 641.
13. In Yost, p. 48; Patton, p. 124. Edmund Wilson had felt "thrilled and troubled" by the play, which provided not only "a bitter treatment of war" but also "a less common sense of the incongruity and cruelty of life, of the precariousness of love perched on a table above the corpses . . ., and renewing its eternal twitter in the silence that succeeded the battle." *The Shores of Light*, pp. 748-49.
14. Foreword to *Contemporary Plays of 1921* (*American*) (Cincinnati, 1922), p. 6.
15. Between December, 1951, and December, 1960, the number of productions—not performances—was 471. Patton, p. 101. This statement has been more recently corroborated, in conversation, by Norma Millay.
16. Alan S. Downer, *Fifty Years of American Drama: 1900-1950* (Chicago, 1951), p. 47.

Notes and References

17. Atkins, pp. 38-40.
18. Cf. Cook, in Yost, pp. 47-48; Agnes Kendrick Gray, *The Measure*, No. 7, September, 1921, p. 18.
19. *New Yorker*, III (February 26, 1927), 61; (March 5, 1927), 68, 69.
20. "Minority Report," in *Minor Prophecies* (New York, 1927), pp. 119-20, 126-29, 134.
21. "English Is Beautiful and Singable," *Musical Observer*, XXVI (October, 1927), 11.
22. Watkins, pp. 38-39; Arthur Hobson Quinn, *A History of the American Drama from the Civil War to the Present Day*, rev. ed. (New York, 1937), II, 148-50; Patton, pp. 159-68.

Chapter Six

1. Davison, p. 678.
2. *First Impressions*, p. 112.
3. Information given in a letter of August 30, 1963.
4. George Sarton, *A History of Science*, II: *Hellenistic Science and Culture in the Last Three Centuries B. C.* (Cambridge, Massachusetts, 1959), p. 39.
5. Wilson, *The Shores of Light*, p. 780.
6. Madeleva, pp. 144, 153.
7. The Arthur Davison Ficke Collection in the Yale University Library. See also Floyd Dell's review of Ficke's *Out of Silence, and Other Poems* in *The Measure*, No. 42, August, 1924, p. 12.
8. The copy in the Arthur Davison Ficke Collection has a few differences of punctuation from the published version: line 12 has a semicolon after *steady*; line 17 a semicolon after *roses*. Line 18 ends with four ellipsis periods, and there is no space between lines 18 and 19. Line 19 has no comma after the second *alone*.
9. In "Tension in Poetry" Allen Tate has a peculiar reference to the poem, which he thinks obscure because it uses mass language to arouse sentimental approval in those who agree with Millay about the execution of Sacco and Vanzetti. He asserts that Massachusetts has illogically caused a drying up of crops. If one accepts Millay's simple metaphor—justice is light—the poem follows logically: justice produces a good society as sunlight produces good crops; under clouds of injustice good crops will not flourish but only destructive things such as quack-grass and mildew, which thrive in wet weather. See Tate, *Collected Essays* (Denver, 1959), pp. 76-77.
10. In Yost, p. 38.
11. Late in 1930 Llewelyn Powys wrote from Steepletop to his sister: "We here have lately been tormented by shooting people. It

has been the open season lasting a fortnight and we have seen no less than 11 stags carried away on the backs of motor cars. It is a shame, if only they would go into the next state they would be safe." *Letters of Llewelyn Powys* (London, 1943), p. 158.

12. *The Shores of Light*, p. 773.

13. *Modern American Poetry* (New York, 1936), p. 484; Mid-Century ed., p. 458.

14. Atkins (p. 200) states (by implication, on the authority of Boissevain) that *Fatal Interview* is "an honest record of immediate experience."

15. British reviewers especially emphasized Millay's modern spirit.

16. Sonnet 3. See also Sonnets 11, 23, 47.

17. Matinicus Island is almost directly south of Camden, Maine, twenty miles out. Beyond Matinicus lies Matinicus Rock, a lonely outpost with a lighthouse. Dorothy Simpson, *The Maine Islands* (Philadelphia, 1960).

18. Cook, in Yost, p. 43.

19. For an analysis of Sonnet 11 see Curley in Bibliography.

20. Millay told Wilson in 1948 that she had lost the first draft of that poem. *The Shores of Light*, pp. 769, 787.

21. With the notation "This sonnet to be italicized," the typescript of "Epitaph" in the Arthur Davison Ficke Collection opens with:

> Have you a townsman somewhere in the crowd,
> To urge the wise, deplore the foolish deed,
> Giving you counsel that you will not heed,
> O Hero? . . . and to groan your wounds aloud?
> A simple citizen and unendowed
> With prophecy, but who would have you freed
> Straightway from error, knowing what's decreed,
> And seeing you too thoughtless and so proud?
> Let him remain in shadow and rehearse
> Your former state, the glories of your line;
> Tell how the gods grew angry, of the curse
> They forged, of how you bled and gave no sign;
> And how these matters went from bad to worse,
> Your sword being mortal and the curse divine.

In the typescript sonnets 3 and 8 do not appear. "What rider spurs him from the darkening east," printed as the final sonnet in *Collected Poems*, was number 7 (thus bringing together poems on Egypt and Nineveh), and was followed by sonnets 12 and 13. The introduction of Sonnet 3 was necessary to move from the time of dinosaurs to the origin of mammalian life; Sonnet 8 added earthquake to the disasters surmounted by Man; and sonnets 12-13 have a better position, after more human development, much later than the primitive time of the "coughing tiger." The most notable textual change is in lines 5-6 of Sonnet 2, which were originally much less distinctive:

Spring passed, and summer came; the sky was blue;
Rain fell and there was fog; the sky was grey.

22. King, p. 144.
23. Wordsworth, Preface to *Lyrical Ballads*.
24. On December 5, 1934, Millay told reporters that she was "disillusioned and embittered." New York *Post*, December 5, 1934, p. 5.
25. The second line of the last quatrain breaks the pattern with tetrameter.
26. In the typescript of this poem in the Arthur Davison Ficke Collection, *Libra* of line 8 replaced *Rigel*, which replaced the original *Vega*.
27. The typescript in the Arthur Davison Ficke Collection has an extra quatrain at the end: "My summer heart, so hot and green,/Why do you shake. What you [*sic*] you seen?/'Nothing, nothing that I know . . ./Only, the tree is shaking so!' " Millay did well to omit these lines; but they reveal her feeling that humanity was in a precarious state.
28. W. R. Benét, p. 279; Louise Bogan, "Conversion into Self," *Poetry*, XLV (February, 1935), 277-78; P. B. Rice, "Edna Millay's Maturity," *Nation*, CXXXIX (November 14, 1934), 568; Cook, in Yost, p. 45; Hildegarde Flanner, "Two Poets: Jeffers and Millay," in *After the Genteel Tradition: American Writers since 1910*, ed. Malcolm Cowley (New York, 1937), p. 165.
29. *Flowers of Evil*, pp. vii, x, xi-xii.
30. "Eleven Words for Seven," *Nation*, CXLIII (July 4, 1936), 22.
31. *Flowers of Evil*, pp. xx, xxiv, xxv. Note also Dillon's "Reply with Rejoinder to Mary Colum's Article 'Edna Millay and Her Time,' " *New Republic*, CXXIV (April 23, 1951), 4.
32. Cf. Arnold Whitridge, "Baudelaire in English," *Yale Review*, n. s., XXV (Summer, 1936), 823; Tate, "Eleven Words for Seven," p. 23.
33. Whitridge, pp. 822, 823.

Chapter Seven

1. "A Diversity of Opinions," *Poetry*, LI (November, 1937), 104.
2. "Give That Beat Again," *The Shores of Light*, p. 684.
3. In a letter to Ficke, November 2, 1938 (in the Arthur Davison Ficke Collection in the Yale University Library), Joseph Freeman suggested a resemblance between *Conversation* and Ficke's *Mr. Faust*. This resemblance is limited to a similarity of scene—a wealthy man's house where a discussion occurs. Millay dedicated the book "To

Arthur Davison Ficke and 42 Commerce Street," the address of Ficke's studio in the early 1920's. Llewelyn Powys knew in November, 1936, of the dedication. *Letters of Llewelyn Powys,* p. 212.

4. Michel Mok, "Poetic Strife Begins at 42 for Edna St. Vincent Millay," New York *Post,* December 5, 1934, p. 5.

5. Clipping from an unidentified newspaper in the W. Adolphe Roberts scrapbook in the Vassar College Library.

6. Patton, pp. 204-6; Bishop, *Poetry,* LI (November, 1937), 101; Thomas Caldecott Chubb, "Shelley Grown Old," *North American Review,* CCXLV (September, 1938), 178.

7. Also the reader suddenly hears Merton defending the Supreme Court as an institution of "scrupulous integrity," regardless of the age of its justices. (57-58) This is one of the passages invented for the second version of the poem, reflecting the controversy over President Roosevelt's Judicial Reorganization Bill introduced February 3, 1937.

8. One should recall the Russian trials and "purges" of August, 1936, and January, 1937.

9. King, p. 150; Patton, pp. 209-10.

10. Patton, pp. 176-92.

11. *Panic* (Boston and New York, 1935), pp. 48-49.

12. Patton, pp. 195-96.

13. *Ibid.,* p. 198.

14. Wilson, *The Shores of Light,* p. 685.

15. One line is "She came by way of Lulworth Cove." A copy of the poem dated April 17, 1934, was sent to Powys with the title "For L. P." from The Cove Hotel, Lulworth Cove, Dorset. It is in the Yale University Library. *Huntsman, What Quarry?* was dedicated to Powys and his wife, Alyse Gregory.

16. Millay discussed the poem with George Dillon; "secret body" instead of "quiet body" was his suggestion. *Letters of Edna St. Vincent Millay,* p. 301.

17. King, pp. 234-35.

18. She mentioned it in a letter to Dillon, March 23, 1939.

19. Paul Rosenfeld, "Under Angry Constellations," *Poetry,* LV (October, 1939), 48.

20. New York *Herald Tribune,* October 25, 1939, p. 11. The United States Neutrality Act was amended November 3, 1939, so as to repeal the embargo on arms.

21. Note of September 4, 1941, on preface to *Collected Sonnets,* in the Arthur Davison Ficke Collection in the Yale University Library.

22. King, p. 227.

23. One suspects that Millay found her imagination stirred on this subject after she made a hurried, brief reply in 1937 or early 1938 to questions from *Books Abroad* about her reading: "Before I was ten

years old, I had read almost every word of Shakespeare. . . . I had also read *Don Quixote*, Christopher Marlowe's *Hero and Leander*, a great deal of Alexander Pope, Grimm's *Fairy Tales*, *Alice in Wonderland*, the poems of Tennyson, Jean Ingelow, and Milton." *Books Abroad*, XII (Spring, 1938), 165.

24. In Yost, p. 54.

25. Louise Townsend Nicholl, "A Late, Rich Harvest of Edna Millay," New York *Herald Tribune Books*, May 23, 1954, p. 5.

26. Breuer, p. 54.

27. Cf. her letter of January 2, 1941, to her classmate Charlotte Babcock Sills.

28. King, pp. 234, 235.

Chapter Eight

1. Millay was accused of self-conscious flippancy, ignoble adroitness, unworthy cuteness, pseudo-sophisticated smartness. See Untermeyer, *American Poetry Since 1900*, p. 217; Kreymborg, *Our Singing Strength*, p. 441; Clement Wood, *Poets of America* (New York, 1925), pp. 203-12; McInnis, p. 424. Sister Madeleva, however, said that Millay had "let a gust of gay and impudent laughter in upon the feverish sentimentalism of the day" (p. 150).

2. Davison, pp. 672-81.

3. Blankenship, p. 626; Parks, pp. 46-48.

4. McInnis, pp. 424-25.

5. Ludwig Lewisohn, *The Story of American Literature* (New York, 1932), p. 580.

6. "Miss Millay's Sonnets," *New Republic*, LXVI (May 6, 1931), 335-36. Tate evidently changed his standards later: the revision of this review in *Reactionary Essays on Poetry and Ideas* (New York, 1936) shows a consistent toning-down of nearly every favorable statement.

7. "The Literary Worker's Polonius," in *The Shores of Light*, p. 605; originally in *Atlantic Monthly* (June, 1935).

8. "Edna St. Vincent Millay, 1892-1950," *Nation*, CLXXI (December 20, 1950), 704.

9. Breuer, p. 50.

10. "Tiger Lily," unpublished memoir in the Vassar College Library, pp. 11, 14.

11. Josephine Miles, *Eras and Modes in English Poetry* (Berkeley, 1964), pp. 27, 261.

12. Floyd Dell, "The Ficke Wing," *The Measure*, No. 42, August, 1924, pp. 12-13.

13. "Miss Millay as Artist," *Nation*, CLIII (December 20, 1941), 644.

14. Scott, p. 340.

15. Hackett, p. 21.

Selected Bibliography

PRIMARY SOURCES

Prefaces and musical settings by Millay are not cited.

1. *Collections of Poetry*

Renascence and Other Poems. New York: Mitchell Kennerley, 1917.
A Few Figs from Thistles. Poems and Four Sonnets. Salvo One. New York: Frank Shay, 1920. Enlarged editions, 1921, 1922.
Second April. New York: Mitchell Kennerley, 1921.
The Harp-Weaver and Other Poems. New York and London: Harper and Brothers, 1923.
The Buck in the Snow. New York and London: Harper and Brothers, 1928.
Edna St. Vincent Millay's Poems Selected for Young People. New York and London: Harper and Brothers, 1929.
Fatal Interview. Sonnets by Edna St. Vincent Millay. New York and London: Harper and Brothers, 1931.
Wine from These Grapes. New York and London: Harper and Brothers, 1934.
Conversation at Midnight. New York and London: Harper and Brothers, 1937.
Huntsman, What Quarry? New York and London: Harper and Brothers, 1939.
Make Bright the Arrows; 1940 Notebook. New York and London: Harper and Brothers, 1940.
Invocation to the Muses. New York and London: Harper and Brothers, 1941.
Collected Sonnets. New York and London: Harper and Brothers, 1941.
The Murder of Lidice. New York and London: Harper and Brothers, 1942.
Collected Lyrics. New York and London: Harper and Brothers, 1943.
Poem and Prayer for an Invading Army. New York: National Broadcasting Company, 1944.
Mine the Harvest. New York and London: Harper and Brothers, 1954.
Collected Poems. New York: Harper and Brothers, 1956.

2. *Plays*

Aria da Capo. First published in *Reedy's Mirror*, March 18, 1920; then in *The Chapbook (A Monthly Miscellany)*, No. 14, August, 1920; then by Mitchell Kennerley, 1921.

Selected Bibliography

The Lamp and the Bell. New York: Frank Shay, 1921.
Two Slatterns and a King. A Moral Interlude. Cincinnati: Stewart Kidd, 1921.
The King's Henchman. New York and London: Harper and Brothers, 1927.
The Princess Marries the Page. New York and London: Harper and Brothers, 1932.

3. *Translations*

"Heavenly and Earthly Love," in *All the Plays of Molnár.* New York: Vanguard Press, 1929.
Flowers of Evil. From the French of Charles Baudelaire, with George Dillon. New York and London: Harper and Brothers, 1936.

4. *Letters*

Letters of Edna St. Vincent Millay. Edited by Allan Ross Macdougall. New York and London: Harper and Brothers, 1952.
BURDEN, JEAN. "With Love from Vincent," *Yankee,* XXII (May, 1958), 40-43, 92-95. Incorporates letters to Millay's aunt, Susan Emery Ricker.
CARPENTER, MARGARET H. *Sara Teasdale.* New York: Schulte Publishing Co., 1960. Letters to and from Millay, pp. 166, 231-32.
LOVE, KENNETT. "The Best-Known Undergraduate," *USA 1,* I (June, 1962), 74. Has a letter of late 1918 to her college friend Katherine Tilt.

5. *Uncollected Writings: Poetry*

(Only items not included by Yost are listed.)
"The Arrival," in *And Spain Sings,* pp. 57-61. Edited by M. J. Bernadete and Rolfe Humphries. New York: Vanguard Press, 1937. Translation of "Llegada" by Emilio Prados.
"The President with a Candidate's Face," New York *Herald Tribune,* November 3, 1940, Sec. II, p. 1.
"Sonnet" [You men and women all of British birth], *The New York Times Magazine,* February 16, 1941, p. 2.
"Not to Be Spotted by His Blood," *The New York Times Magazine,* December 28, 1941, p. 5.
"Thanksgiving, 1942," *The New York Times Magazine,* November 22, 1942, pp. 5-6.
"For My Brother Han and My Sisters, in Holland," *The New York Times Magazine,* January 7, 1945, p. 24.
"To the Leaders of the Allied Nations," *The New York Times Magazine,* January 21, 1945.

"Thanksgiving . . . 1950," *Saturday Evening Post*, CCXXIII (November 25, 1950), 31.

6. *Uncollected Writings: Prose*

(Only items not included by Yost are listed.)

"My Debt to Books," *Books Abroad*, XII (Spring, 1938), 165.

"The Little Boy Next Door," *Talks* . . . *A Quarterly Digest of Addresses . . . Broadcast over the Columbia Network*, VI (April, 1941), 6. An appeal to feed Chinese children.

"Nothing . . . If Not Enough," *This Week Magazine*, February 7, 1943, p. 2. Encouragement to continue war effort.

SECONDARY SOURCES

1. *Bibliographies*

American Literary Manuscripts. Austin: University of Texas Press, 1960.

BRENNI, VITO J., and JOHN E. JAMES. "Edna St. Vincent Millay: Selected Criticism," *Bulletin of Bibliography*, XXIII (May-August, 1962), 177-78. Lists more than 100 critical essays and reviews. Not always accurate.

KOHN, JOHN S. VAN E. "Some Undergraduate Printings of Edna St. Vincent Millay," *Publisher's Weekly*, CXXXVIII (November 30, 1940), 2026-29.

MILLETT, FRED B. *Contemporary American Authors*. New York: Harcourt, Brace and Co., 1943.

SPILLER, ROBERT E., WILLARD THORP, THOMAS H. JOHNSON, and HENRY SEIDEL CANBY. *Literary History of the United States*, III. Bibliography, pp. 656-58. Supplement, pp. 169-70. New York: Macmillan and Co., 1962.

TATE, ALLEN (ed.). *Sixty American Poets, 1896-1944*. Revised Edition. Washington: The Library of Congress, 1954, pp. 85-89.

YOST, KARL. *A Bibliography of the Works of Edna St. Vincent Millay*. New York: Harper and Brothers, 1937. Inadequate regarding secondary material but indispensable for primary material through 1936.

2. *Material in Books*

(Since Miriam Gurko's *Restless Spirit* contains an excellent bibliography, very few items pertaining to Millay's biography are listed.)

ATKINS, ELIZABETH. *Edna St. Vincent Millay and Her Times*. Chicago: The University of Chicago Press, 1936. An excessively adulatory

Selected Bibliography

work diluted by irrelevant literary history; but comments on individual works are sometimes perceptive.

BLANKENSHIP, RUSSELL. *American Literature as an Expression of the National Mind.* New York: Henry Holt & Co., 1931. Sees Millay as a superb, essentially unphilosophical singer of the joy of living. (Not cited by Yost.)

BRENNER, RICA. *Ten Modern Poets.* New York: Harcourt, Brace and Co., 1930. Indicates the poet's early bent for humor and parody.

CARGILL, OSCAR. *Intellectual America: Ideas on the March.* New York: Macmillan and Co., 1941. Though he thinks Millay influenced for the worse by decadence, and carelessly contributing to the moral chaos of the 1920's, he praises much and gives her credit for helping to free America from irrational taboos.

COOK, HAROLD LEWIS. "Edna St. Vincent Millay,—An Essay," in *A Bibliography of the Works of Edna St. Vincent Millay,* ed. KARL YOST. New York: Harper and Brothers, 1937. He thinks the conservatism of woman is behind the poet's lack of analysis, her conclusiveness, her intimate presentation of warm life. He commends her accuracy, mastery of sonnet form, and breaking through restrictions placed on women writers. Millay commended Cook for understanding her poetry in "a thoughtful and lucid study."

[DELL, FLOYD]. "Edna St. Vincent Millay," *The Literary Spotlight.* New York: George H. Doran Co., 1924. Perceptive regarding the multiplicity of Millay's nature, and her affectations.

EASTMAN, MAX. "My Friendship with Edna Millay," *Great Companions: Critical Memoirs of Some Famous Friends.* New York: Farrar, Straus and Cudahy, 1959. Valuable concerning Eastman's friendship with Millay and her husband during the 1920's and 1930's.

GURKO, MIRIAM. *Restless Spirit: The Life of Edna St. Vincent Millay.* New York: Thomas Y. Crowell Co., 1962. Good biography, addressed especially to readers of high-school age. Emphasizes Millay's volatility and elusiveness as a subject; contains excellent bibliography relating to the poet's life.

KREYMBORG, ALFRED. *Our Singing Strength.* New York: Coward-McCann, Inc., 1929. Comments on individual poems. (Not cited by Yost.)

LOGGINS, VERNON. *I Hear America . . . Literature in the United States Since 1900.* New York: Thomas Y. Crowell Co., 1937. Rapid but discriminating review. Millay still a minor poet.

MADELEVA, SISTER M. "Where Are You Going, My Pretty Maid?" *Chaucer's Nuns and Other Essays.* New York: D. Appleton and Co., 1925. Shrewd, level-headed assessment of Millay's poetic successes, weaknesses, and potentialities up to 1925.

SHAFTER, TOBY. *Edna St. Vincent Millay, America's Best-Loved Poet.* New York: Julian Messner, 1957. Inaccurate and inadequate work for juvenile readers.

SHEEAN, VINCENT. *The Indigo Bunting: A Memoir of Edna St. Vincent Millay.* New York: Harper and Brothers, 1951. Throws light on Millay's way of life and interests in the 1940's, especially her long-continued interest in birds.

UNTERMEYER, LOUIS. *American Poetry since 1900.* New York: Harcourt, Brace and Co., 1923. Praises Millay's intensity, capacity for ecstasy, and felicity of language; disparages facile cynicism of *A Few Figs.*

VAN DOREN, CARL. "Youth and Wings: Edna St. Vincent Millay," *Many Minds.* New York: Alfred A. Knopf, 1924. Appreciative analysis.

WILSON, EDMUND. "Epilogue, 1952: Edna St. Vincent Millay," *The Shores of Light: A Literary Chronicle of the Twenties and Thirties.* New York: Farrar, Straus and Young, Inc., 1952. A significant account of personal acquaintance during Greenwich Village period and of some later encounters, especially near the end of Millay's life.

3. *Unpublished Studies*

KING, GRACE HAMILTON. *The Development of the Social Consciousness of Edna St. Vincent Millay as Manifested in Her Poetry.* Dissertation. New York University, 1943. Millay's social consciousness was initiated through reading, furthered by Greenwich Village experiences, the Sacco-Vanzetti case, and the rise of Fascism and Communism. Important because it contains Millay's views expressed in an interview of 1941.

PATTON, JOHN JOSEPH. *Edna St. Vincent Millay as a Verse Dramatist.* Dissertation. University of Colorado, 1962. Ann Arbor, Michigan: University Microfilms, Inc., No. 63-2006. A thorough study which gives Millay much credit for perpetuating verse drama with six effective plays.

PETITT, JEAN MORRIS. *Edna St. Vincent Millay: A Critical Study of Her Poetry in Its Social and Literary Milieu.* Dissertation. Vanderbilt University, 1955. Ann Arbor, Michigan: University Microfilms, Inc., Doctoral Dissertation Series, No. 15,799. Though it contains many annoying slips and the author is insensitive to much of Millay's best work, it provides some understanding of the literary milieu. Asserts that the poet had strong religious faith and that her poetry, in its intense emotionality, is that of the last American Romantic.

Selected Bibliography

4. Articles, Essays, and Reviews

BENÉT, WILLIAM ROSE. "Round About Parnassus," *Saturday Review of Literature*, XI (November 10, 1934), 279. On *Wine from These Grapes*. Finds evidence of development.

BREUER, ELIZABETH. "Edna St. Vincent Millay," *Pictorial Review*, XXXIII (November, 1931), 2. An excellent account of Steepletop life, Millay's habits and attitudes, and the philosophy of her marriage.

COLUM, PADRAIC. "Miss Millay's Poems," *The Freeman*, IV (November 2, 1921), 189-90. Judicious assigning of praise and blame which distinguishes between childlike and mature.

CURLEY, FRANCIS X. "Edna St. Vincent Millay," *America*, LXXXIV (November 11, 1950), 166-68. Praise of sharp observation of nature, craftsmanship, and sincerity in *Fatal Interview* (with detailed analysis of Sonnet XI).

DABBS, JAMES MCBRIDE. "Edna St. Vincent Millay: Not Resigned," *South Atlantic Quarterly*, XXXVII (January, 1938), 54-66. An interesting analysis that takes Millay to task for lacking resignation but eventually finds her forced to write as she has done because of her situation in respect to religious tradition.

DAVISON, EDWARD. "Edna St. Vincent Millay," *English Journal*, XVI (1927), 671-82. Though placing her high among her American contemporaries, he confines the poet to a relatively minor position. Objects to the sensational, seamy, and flippant in her work, praises fine lyrics but thinks Millay has no consistent scheme of values by which to measure the world, and thus cannot achieve greatness.

DuBOIS, A. E. "Edna St. Vincent Millay," *Sewanee Review*, XLIII (1935), 80-104. A penetrating psychological analysis showing Millay as a combination of precocious and spoiled child, pure poet, woman, and mystic. (Not cited by Yost.)

GREGORY, HORACE. "Edna St. Vincent Millay, Poet and Legend," New York *Herald Tribune Books*, November 11, 1934, p. 3. On *Wine from These Grapes*.

HACKETT, FRANCIS. "Edna St. Vincent Millay," *New Republic*, CXXXV (December 24, 1956), 21-22. Tribute to Millay's greatness, focused on *Collected Poems*. Her poetry expresses desire for emancipation, scorn of evasion, a large sense of America, reverence for life and indignation at its abuse. She explores the tragic sense of our time.

HAY, SARA HENDERSON. "The Unpersuadable V," *Saturday Review*, XXXVII (June 5, 1954), 20. Good summary of Millay's most important qualities.

HILL, FRANK ERNEST. "Edna St. Vincent Millay," *The Measure*, No. 1 (March, 1921), pp. 25-26. On *A Few Figs from Thistles*. Points out the dominance of the dramatic in Millay's work. (Not cited by Yost.)

McINNIS, EDGAR. "The New Writers—Edna St. Vincent Millay," *Canadian Forum*, XI (August, 1931), 424-25. Finds Millay's work uneven, best when she combines simplicity and sincerity in her less experimental poetry.

MONROE, HARRIET. "Advance or Retreat?" *Poetry*, XXXVIII (July, 1931), 216-21. On *Fatal Interview*.

————. "Edna St. Vincent Millay," *Poetry*, XXIV (August, 1924), 260-66. Emphasizes Millay's truthfulness and sincerity, with special praise for her sonnets.

O'F., S. "Literature and Life. Edna St. Vincent Millay," *The Irish Statesman*, XII (1929), 213-14. Finds *The Buck in the Snow* mature, like Yeats of middle period; praises her technical ability, her use of homely image and simple word. (Not cited by Yost.)

PARKS, EDD WINFIELD. "Edna St. Vincent Millay," *Sewanee Review*, XXXVIII (January, 1930), 42-49. Thinks Millay, a poet of beautiful but narrow range, emotional and unphilosophical, has been moved by the discipline of writing *The King's Henchman* and by the Sacco-Vanzetti affair to more experimental techniques, more objective poetry, and perhaps to becoming a greater, more philosophical poet.

PRESTON, JOHN H. "Edna St. Vincent Millay," *Virginia Quarterly Review*, III (1927), 342-55. Strong approval of Millay's sensuous paganism, nearness to elemental things, and especially *The King's Henchman* and the sonnets.

RANSOM, JOHN CROWE. "The Poet as Woman," *Southern Review*, II (Spring, 1937), 783-806. Reprinted in *The World's Body*. New York and London: Charles Scribner's Sons, 1938. Exposes some of Atkins' inadequacies; thinks Millay lacking in intellectual interest, too unlike Donne, but typically a woman artist. Unintentionally patronizing.

RICHART, BETTE. "Poet of Our Youth," *Commonweal*, LXVI (May 10, 1957), 150-51. Typical of late unfavorable views: thinks Millay usually neurotic, shrill, and juvenile except in sonnets.

SCHWARTZ, DELMORE. "Poetry of Millay," *Nation*, CLVII (December 19, 1943), 735-36. Representative of unfavorable views of the 1940's: condemns lack of growth and poems' being derived from reading.

SCOTT, NATHAN A. J. "Millay: A Reconsideration," *Christian Century*, LXXIV (May 1, 1957), 559-60. Self-preoccupation condemned

Selected Bibliography

Millay to youthful lyricism; she failed to bridge the gap between private and public worlds.

SCOTT, WINFIELD TOWNLEY. "Millay Collected," *Poetry*, LXIII (March, 1944), 334-42. Millay's work suffers from repetitiousness, self-pity, sentimentality, overdone emotion, and loss of humor; but she always had integrity, and much of her poetry shows sharp observation, power, and passion.

TAGGARD, GENEVIEVE. "A Woman's Anatomy of Love," New York *Herald Tribune Books*, April 19, 1931, p. 3. On *Fatal Interview*. Praises Millay as a traditional writer, accounts for her special success in sonnets.

TATE, ALLEN. "Miss Millay's Sonnets," *New Republic*, LXVI (May 6, 1931), 335-36. (A systematically modified version of this is in *Reactionary Essays on Poetry and Ideas*. New York: Charles Scribner's Sons, 1936.) Finds Millay a distinguished poet of the second rank (a sensibility, not an intellect) who created a personal idiom from traditional symbols and nineteenth-century vocabulary. *Fatal Interview* a very skillful sustained performance in the Shakespearean form.

WATKINS, MARY F. "Operatic Events of the Past Month," *The Musical Observer*, XXVI (April, 1927), 12, 38-39. The most informative early assessment of *The King's Henchman*. (Not cited by Yost.)

Index

DATE DUE

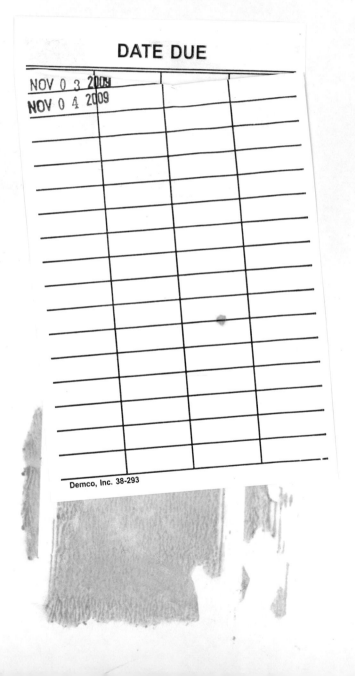

NOV 0 3 2009			
NOV 0 4 2009			

Demco, Inc. 38-293